MAKE IT TRUE
POETRY FROM CASCADIA

MAKE IT TRUE

POETRY FROM CASCADIA

EDITED BY

PAUL NELSON   GEORGE STANLEY

BARRY MCKINNON   NADINE MAESTAS

leaf press

Library and Archives Canada Cataloguing in Publication

Make it true : poems from Cascadia / editors, George Stanley, Barry McKinnon, Paul Nelson, Nadine Maestas.

ISBN 978-1-926655-81-9 (pbk.)

1. Canadian poetry (English)--Northwest, Pacific. 2. American poetry--Northwest, Pacific. 3. Canadian poetry (English)--21st century. 4. American poetry--21st century. I. Stanley, George, 1934-, editor II. McKinnon, Barry, 1944-, editor III. Nelson, Paul, 1961-, editor IV. Maestas, Nadine, 1976-, editor

PS8295.5.B7M34 2015   C811'.608097111   C2015-902091-3

The cover image is of salmon swimming under the highway entering/leaving Nanaimo. This underpass serves as shelter and refuge for many homeless people. Salmon populate all corners of Cascadia; they swim away and then home again, navigating the rivers and creeks through and under our cities and towns without most people even noticing.

We are grateful to Justin Kaczmarek, the artist who painted *Salmon Run,* for permission to use the image. His helpers were Cadence Warner, Logan Ford, Tyler Sexsmith and Jeanne Ironside.

Kim Goldberg gave permission to use her photographs of the salmon mural. That panorama, a creative work in itself, would not now be possible to replicate, because the mural has been degraded over time.

Thanks also to Five Fathom Studios for their expertise. To Joanne Baumann for help with research. And to the City of Nanaimo, for helping bring this art and this book together.

The editors have allowed the poets from south of the straight line their eccentric spelling.

This book is set in Warnock Pro and Cronos Pro. The cover title is Raincoat, a typeface that describes itself as having secret Victorian roots and a rock-and-roll heart.

Printed in Canada on FSC certified papers.

Leaf Press
PO Box 416
Lantzville, BC, Canada
www.leafpress.ca
V0R 2H0

TABLE OF CONTENTS ❧

INTRODUCTION ❧

I was delighted to be reminded recently of the fact that the roots of the word essay are French, *essayer*, to examine, to test, embark upon, attempt. In that light, this anthology itself may be seen as sort of an essay on the bioregion lying west of the continental divide, spanning from Cape Mendocino in the south to Mt. Logan in the north. An attempt to discover the cultural mores unique to Cascadia and create greater awareness of them in the bioregion for the express purpose of deepening the sense of place. Part of a cultural investigation by which we learn as we go about the place in which we live so that we may inhabit it as if we knew our lives and livelihoods were inextricably entwined with those of every other being. It is an attempt to resuscitate the poetry culture from the trance cast by the pop/consumer/industry-generated culture—an anti-culture which, as Edward Abbey understood, serves to consume everything, including the biosphere: "Growth for the sake of growth is the ideology of the cancer cell."

And this anthology is assembled with the assumption that it is the poetry outsiders who are forward-looking and have the best chance at deepening that cultural animation. The marginalized (for whatever reason) poets are the harshest critics of conventional wisdom in culture and in bioregional poetry culture; the best of them also serve the poet's traditional function as prophet. This book's organizing principles of what is open and outside, with subsets of what is experimental and challenging, are related to George Stanley's proposition stated at the second Cascadia Poetry Festival in May 2014 in Seattle: that contemporary poetry faces the tyranny of the ironic; so making it new again means responding to the cultural situation in 2015, similar to the way Modernists responded to theirs circa 1912 and the Postmodernists in 1960 with the New American Poetry, and going deeper than the ironic. From the earlier Modernist push (and Ezra Pound) we get our title, slightly paraphrased, Make It True. As a person of Cuban descent, I also resonate with poet José Lezama Lima's notion that "only the difficult is stimulating," but difficulty is not easy to communicate and that which appears simple on the surface may have depths a quick reading or two may not reveal.

So bioregionalism, or the effort to reimagine ourselves and the places where we live in terms of ecology, sustainability and harmony with the natural systems, is a huge part of what guides us and what inspired the idea behind the creation of this book. It may be that we can be bioregionalists more easily here. Few places on earth are blessed with the same kind of mountains, volcanos, islands, fjords, waterfalls, hot springs, glaciers, thousands of miles of coastline, rain forests, ancient trees and other natural features. These features are easy to recognize as inspired creations well worth preserving, protecting and venerating, especially, in George Bowering's words, "in this time of the easily awesome." Threats to basic survival are becoming quite real now that irreversible climate changes are beginning to manifest. The tenets of bioregionalism have gained traction in the forty-plus years since the term was coined, and it is simply a matter of time that we protect the biosphere bioregion by bioregion or face continued extinction, perhaps of the human species. The world of particulars, so well represented in the two previous poetry moments referenced above, begin to trump abstractions like flags and nations. We heed the prophecy of Tu Fu who saw that nations would be destroyed but mountains and rivers would remain. In fact we look to Asia more readily here in Cascadia than we'd look to Europe, as Kenneth Rexroth recognized seventy years ago, while we also take from traditional indigenous cultures the examples of how to best inhabit this place. At its core bioregionalism is about positive action, urban sustainability and restoring watersheds. Modern culture is so separated from the natural world, learning what our watersheds are in most urban areas would be progress.

Bioregionalism is also about opposition to the great corporate monoculture, Disney McWorld some would have it, as expressed in Jared Leising's poem Keep Portland Weird, while celebrating the vast wilderness expressed in Sarah de Leeuw's Skeena. In fact wilderness itself is an organizing principle of the book, as the editors are open and perhaps partial to the wilderness of the mind as expressed in many of the poems published here. See Lary Timewell's molecular hyperbole in which he suggests poetry is: ": the mind already in the afterlife; : an Ipanema of toilsome derivatives; : retrograde expressions still smoking in the shadows; : hybrid music that can now no longer go nameless; : autobiography of the imagination, first draft" and even ": a replicated marvel done in slightly more expensive crayons," among other wildly imaginative things.

In fact it is the wilderness of the mind that may need protecting most of all in our industry-generated-culture/gadget-addled society where Diane di Prima's warning that the only war that matters is the war against the imagination and that all other wars are subsumed in it is prophetic. Is the push to violence and the need to resolve conflict via violence a failure of the imagination? Surely. That and an inability to communicate, though, as with abstract expressionist painter Clyfford Still, "Demands for communication are presumptuous and irrelevant." The best art communicates with what it doesn't say, with what it implies and even with the field that it emits, transmission being an ancient way of getting knowledge from one party to another.

But in Cascadia there are other ways that engage and use the imagination, separate and distinct from other bioregions in North America, certainly. How the peaceful joint occupancy of San Juan Island for twelve years before it was decided that it (and several other nearby islands) were to be part of the US and not what would become Canada is a telling example of how the old ways don't seem to work here as well. A war over the boundary dispute was avoided, and the gut hunch is that there is something about this place that creates an environment where a violent solution is untenable, or rare. Culturally, the San Juan Islands have always been part of Cascadia. Perhaps that aspect of this place is due to the Indigenous presence that had nowhere else to go once the settlers got to the West Coast. Perhaps it is because most of British Columbia (and therefore a huge percentage of Cascadia) was unceded by First Peoples. Maybe it is due to the geographical situation of being on the Pacific Rim and looking west to Asia and being closer to Asian culture than to European culture that is what sets Cascadia apart.

One clear way to begin to reinhabit is to practice of a mode of writing evocative of what Robin Blaser in his seminal essay called the "practice of outside." It is a method born here and still informing the best of Cascadia poets seeking to create a gesture that is from here and taps into forces that surely must still be here, resonances of cultures that once lived sustainably in this place. As Chief Seattle put it, *This place is swarming with the invisible dead of my tribe.*

The accessible Zen push of poets like Jim Dodge and Sam Hamill is included here. Dodge would prefer the phrase "tectonic existentialism." Those who believe there is liberation in learning the proper names for things. Hamill suggests: "When Master K'ung says, 'All wisdom is rooted in learning to call things (including ideas and emotions) by their right names,' the exactitude of a poet's work takes on a new dimension." There is also a generous sampling here of the legacy of the bioregion's most seminal poetry event, the 1963 Vancouver Poetry Conference. George Bowering, Daphne Marlatt, Fred Wah, Jamie Reid and Judith Copithorne are included, along with many poets inspired by their work and experiments. We have worked hard to get as wide a geographical diversity as possible, with poets from Alaska to Arcata, from Nanaimo to Missoula, with the understanding that this is a preliminary effort that will lead to the discovery of other bioregional poets who value the wilderness of the mind and are attempting to go, in Lissa Wolsak's words, more "deeply down their own throats." We included at least one expatriate, Lisa Robertson, who wrote: "I am very pleased to be perceived as Cascadian."

And we give credit to previous attempts to document poets from here, which were formalist in nature, or which preferred references to wilderness more than the wilderness of the mind to which we are partial, or insisted on using the term Pacific Northwest, a phrase which comes across as imperialistic, given that Vancouver and Victoria, two of the main cities in Cascadia, are in Southwest Canada, as George Bowering was happy to shout out from the seats of a panel during Cascadia II, for good reason. *Pacific Northwestern Spiritual Poetry, On Sacred Ground, Long Journey, Alive at the Center* and a recent Cascadia edition of *Manoa Journal* covered ground that we don't have to cover. There are few poets common to both this book and those previous publications, though the influence of Sam Hamill and Judith Roche especially could not be ignored, influence being another organizing principle of the book.

Attempts at an Articulation of a Bioregional Poetics

One take on a bioregional poetics comes from extreme Southern Cascadia. We have endeavored to cast a wide net through networking rather than an open call, and south of Portland the pickings get a little slim. Jim Dodge, one of the long-time figures in the south, has also been part of the bioregional movement since nearly its inception. A lifetime of bioregional thinking and poetry practice resulted in this informal missive he sent with the understanding that he can't claim ownership of all the notions expressed and that ideas and influences "tend to run together":

Bioregional Poetics/Aesthetics: Some Tentative Tenets

1. The bioregional aesthetic is community-based, and yields completely to the central precept that community is not limited to the human, but includes all the flora and fauna, the core "cycles of sustenance" (like the water-cycle, or carbon-cycle), and the larger "figures of regulation" (geological forces like plate tectonics, solar income, air and oceanic currents, and other biospheric forces and phenomena). The overarching principle informing bioregional poetics is sometimes called the "biocentric" or "ecological" view, where life in all its forms and myriad relationships is central to all aesthetic considerations. This paradigm of existence is obviously and staunchly opposed to the prevailing viewpoints of the "anthropocentric" (human centered) or "egocentric" (centered on the individual human psyche, also known as a self). When fossil sea lilies were

discovered near the peak of Mount Everest, we started calling bioregionalism "tectonic existentialism," and laughed at ourselves for having the temerity to call it anything.

2. The bioregion is the body of metaphor. To communicate, art requires a shared set of references, sources held in common. In constructing associations where you're trying to embody the ineffable (like love, say, or deep regard), the more familiar the vehicle, the finer the understanding. So if you say love is a bird, most people who have seen a bird sense the associations of bird: flight/freedom; nest/home-safety-nurture; song: joy/peace. Even more precise, of course, is to specify the bird (love is a falcon) or bird and activity (love is a falcon turning in a widening gyre). To communicate completely, it is most helpful to actually KNOW the referent,

to live it. (Love is a ruby-throated hummingbird fumbling the foxglove's flower-heads, the thrum of its wings reverberating in the throats of the pitcher plants along the boggy plains of the Smith River.) Maybe it's flogging the obvious, but the more a reader or viewer shares the creator's references, the higher the quality of communication. In that sense, all poetry is local. Or poetry is all locale.

3. The bioregion is the home of the vernacular. Bioregional poetics conceives of language as a living, wild system, and of poems as similarly dynamic systems of complex associations. Because bioregional poetics is virtually founded on the notion that the power, point, and animating purpose of poetry is high-quality communication, the poetics almost demands a commitment to the vernacular as the primary mode of expression. In the usual sense of "the vernacular," this means a commitment to the "everyday language of the people" as spoken or otherwise used in informal discourse and communication, as opposed to formal or official discourse. It embraces idiom, local locutions, and the common and ordinary style with the same fervor that it eschews the specialized and pretentious. Above all, the poetics values accessibility and inclusion; it wants to communicate with the community and to offer its connections and associations with clarity and grace, leading to understanding, appreciation, and communion.

4. Bioregional poetics serves to mediate human culture and ecosystems/ bioregion/biosphere. It is a tool to explore relationships and associations in life as it is lived. Further, it extends individual identity to include "the sum of sustaining relationships"—everything from family genetics to the food one eats, including the modes of subsistence. Since the exploration is communal, bioregional poets and artists display a strong sense of community and cooperation and tend to minimize the scrimmages of ego that mark so many literary movements. They hold to Jack Spicer's view that we are all working on the same poem, singing the same song, telling the same story, and that the primary responsibility of community artists is to do their part to the utmost of their abilities, to encourage the best in each other, and to let posterity decide—as it does anyway—who will be remembered. As Spicer admonishes in his "The Future of American Poetry II," citing his grandmother's advice, ". . .when you get in a fight with a dog turd, you only get shit on your fingers."

5. A bioregional poetics in no way supposes a closed, provincial aesthetics. On the contrary, the natural world teaches the importance of being eminently open to all influences, since diversity offers the greatest flexibility in the dance of adaptation, not to mention the surest footing on the Cliffs of Despair. If you live in the Pacific Northwest, for example, geographically you are part of the Pacific Rim configuration, and thus subject to the

influences of Japanese and Chinese philosophy and religion, the Hispanic and Latin American cultures on the southern borderlands, and American culture in general through mass media that are part and parcel of quickly evolving technologies. We have more information than we can know, and what knowledge we think we possess deserves a deeper reflection than time seems to allow. In an age where wisdom may well reside in believing nothing you hear and only half of what you see in the storm of electronic transmissions and babbling bloggers, watching the big maple on a nearby ridge bow to the wind may be information you can build a truth on. The old scout's adage holds particularly dear as we're bombarded with fuzzy claims and distant factoids: "The closer you get to the source, the less likely something has crapped upstream."

Some brief thoughts about Dodge's notes. That he sees bioregional poetics as "biocentric" rings true with me, regardless of the bioregion, but is especially resonant here and is also indicative of the greater appreciation/application of Asian wisdom cultures. I'd single out Hua-yen Buddhism, which has been described as the "interdependent origination of the universe," as a forerunner to the notions of bioregionalism and the biocentric approach. For me this also evokes Blaser's poetics and the notion of the practice of outside. The notion of responses to the Anthropocene also informs the work and activism of Stephen Collis. Collis was arrested and hit with a SLAPP lawsuit for trespassing in a park attempting to prevent Kinder Morgan's field studies to assess the feasibility of an underground tunnel for the last leg of its proposed Edmonton-to-Burnaby pipeline to transport oil from the tar sands project in Alberta. (A suit that was eventually dropped.) Were the biocentric model first in our consciousness, the tar sands project and fossil fuel projects like it would not even be considered, and people espousing it would likely get mental health care.

Dodge's twist on the local, suggesting "poetry is all locale," is a large part of the depth and lasting legacy of the TISH poetry movement in Canada, which was influenced by Olson, Duncan, Levertov and other US poets. Bowering is clear that one of his gleanings from these poets was to make the poetry local, to have it come out of place, which explains why TISH, in large part, did as much as any movement in Cascadia to foment a bioregional poetics. Marlatt also points out that how the poem is laid out on the page is related to locale. How a poet situates each line, or cluster of lines (stanzas) in relation to other lines, although the failure of e-books to properly represent field poetry is still an issue.

That bioregional poetics would employ the demotic and err on the side of inclusion are points I would agree on; the notions of accessibility and communication are points, at very least, I would question, as suggested by the Still quote above. The notion of composition by field assumes that meaning(s) vary from reader to reader, and the effective capture and conveyance of the energy of events that inspired the poem are just as likely to affect the experience of the poem, if not more so, than any attempt at communicating a specific message. Olson called the poem written this way a "high energy construct." Regardless, the argument about what a poem should communicate, if anything, is not limited to this bioregion, but inspiration from (or reaction to) Blaser, Duncan and Jack Spicer's poetics continues to be the mainstream of the radical poetics from Cascadia.

Dodge's notion of inspiration, ranging from "family genetics to the food one eats, including the modes of subsistence" is critical for many reasons: the depth of the force of personal mythology, the sympathy to projects that can be seen as aspects of bioregionalism—the 100 mile diet; craft beers; regional cuisines (have we mentioned kale yet?)—and do give us a road map away from the extraction economy that is part of the industrial model and the main force destroying the biosphere. This is particularly critical here, because the extraction model continues to wreak havoc (especially in rural Cascadia) and the biomass is less destroyed here than in most other bioregions in the industrial world.

As for Dodge's last point, open is without question the main organizing aspect of this book. I use that term in the same sense Keats used the phrase "negative capability," and there is pressure from each political (and social) pole to close things in, cut off debate, limit options and—in general—narrow the bandwidth. His use of the term diversity is also critical from the point of view that envisioned and edited this book, but the main emphasis is geographic diversity, with aesthetic, ethnic and gender diversity all following.

So while we love the notion of a gesture that transcends anthropocentrism, we see the wilderness of the mind as also beyond that. How that quality is recognized is up for discussion. We would also question what we've come to know as "accessibility." One human's precise clarity is another's incoherence. Those reading the "inaccessible" poems in this book might find something in them that speaks to them beyond an ability to understand what exactly "they mean."

In Northern Cascadia, as far as Prince George, where Barry McKinnon has been toiling for nearly that same time period, the notion he expresses comes out of a tradition in which accessibility is not as much the concern and the notion of subject is even less certain. In an essay he wrote about one of his poems:

> The composing principle for Arrhythmia, and I hope all of my work, was in line with W.C. Williams' dictum that each poem must sum up the poet's life to that point. I wrote Arrhythmia daily with the sense that if I had anything more to say I'd better get at it. If the word "subject" is still in the post-modern lexicon, I believe the poet's subject is time—and that language discloses the actualities therein. Emotion is the poem's fact.

Farther south, Daphne Marlatt would suggest, again going back forty years previous to this writing, that her

> first concern is with language, locus for event. That whatever "themes" exist are arrived at through language—recognized in that sense. Since whatever is known (expressible) is known in language, the poem becomes a way of recognizing or realizing the world, both inner & outer. What kind of ground we walk on, whose air we breathe. That the ecological principle in words forming one or many phrases runs whatever lies outside & forms also what we see—to say... Verse (free verse, laid out with spaces indicating pauses) locates.

This does not sound like a poetry that has accessibility as one of its prime directives. That is even less so with a poet like Lissa Wolsak who suggests:

> ~ Language carries with it a sense of its own descriptive inadequacy and is inspired, when cleavage between active speech and reception of speech merge into unity, however momentary...

while also understanding that "language exceeds speech." Or as I said to Judith Roche about the kind of poetry we prefer, that it "says something without saying something." That communicates without being didactic, or through a tone or, in general, a field.

How to merge the backpacking poet's love of nature expressed through knowledge of the wilderness with the non-backpacker's love of the mind's wilderness and its unconventional (inaccessible? less accessible?) maneuvers? This is a simplification, perhaps, but the view here is closer to the center of the bioregion, albeit still closer to the coast than the exact center.

Ultimately the best of the poems herein have an exactness of naming and imagery, the light of the mind Diane di Prima recognized as "intellectus" along with the wildness of the mind Charles Olson would suggest was a use of speech at its "least careless and least logical." They sing, or they baffle. They inspire and/or they reveal. They are among the best poets practicing here in this place today, as best we could gather as a starting point for discussion and for the effort to remember (or imagine) what it is to BE somewhere. To live here as if we again venerated this place and all its marvelous interconnected systems.

Paul E. Nelson

N.17.14, Feb.23.15

Seattle, WA

CHRISTINE LOWTHER ❧

Nuu-Chah-Nulth, Good Advice

I've been told it's time
to decolonize my mind,
that all the places I love
carry the wrong rhymes:
Lone Cone, Frank Island,
Catface, Colnett:
dubbed by and for
missionaries, Kingdom-come,
imposing replacement.

Ts'ix-wat-sats, Chitaape
Waa naa chuus
Hilth hoo iss:
more than pretty names,
words that came up out of the ground,
as the loon learns his song from the lake.

Try to cover a mountain in concrete?
Language keeps emerging,
the planet speaking its green poems.
The kind of petrifaction in pavement—
the newcomers postpone mortality
preserve everything in hard grey
stop death by spreading it—
lacks logic.
Listen for green,
learn the names.

I've been advised not to study
French or Spanish, rather
to stand still, make roots from words,
take in the language of the place
I've made my home.

DAVID ABEL ☙

from **"Sweep"**

272

We go to work by bus or by car or by train
We buy a washing machine or we do not
We work in the textile industry or we work in some other specific industry
We put a road along one route or we put it along another

We can extend the drunk
and her dog example
to illustrate multiple cointegrating relationships,
cointegrated meanderings

the independence of irrelevant alternatives
(a strong assumption)

make the guess for which the observed data are least surprising

275

Walking, in a storm, on a dull mountain path is not a relaxation
(is more like a reason for being).

279

kollodi's formula:

> word
> shape of word
> sound of word
> image

Friedrich's "relative nonarbitrariness":
Is there anything in speech as arbitrary as the order of the alphabet?

(the shape of the mouth?)

every third thought is my grave

285

Greta Garbo, Civil Rights, Canceled

Tape can be paper or plastic,
staples just another form of wire
to stitch with. What have you

been sewing. "I miss you"
is called "Ignoring the cat
in the crack

between one job and the next."
You're mixed up in my mind,
you two,

back when the arc of a stuck,
no, struck
ball shared that airspace of A.

Whose Panoptic History of Smudges,
whose Catalogue of Erased Messages,
whose Factsheet on Memory Solvents

St Ave
Here in OR

286

I'm in love
with the girl
who was never here to see
the table in the corner
abandoned
by the maté drinker
I would have been
if only someone had given me
the right books
sooner

288

Black Peony

natural sewing

289

My perversions, addictions,
save my life—prolong it—
by redirecting current
through varying circuit paths
so that I don't burn out

Do I believe that?

(Does it matter?)

293

the presence between
nothings
...
given a broom, you of course
sweep

298

Language is love—until it is entered by lies

afeared

Don't you be   — not whilst I'm here, by granny! "An' I can't
understand why, onless it was they was   I couldn't keep a
secret." What I'm   of is mebbe you done the job too well."
"I was   you'd change your mind about marryin' Jack." Ain't
you ?"   "I was   Girty hed your friends, the sisters, an'
mebbe your brother, too. Then he said: "We was all   you'd
kick the stuffin's out of him! An' I'm   he'll burn us out—he's
crazy on fires, anyway—or do somethin' like." He was   we'd
come across an' git the boat thet night. But you needn't be   if
he does." We kinder was   ..."An' bein' a leetle   he might
have come tew harm," the other horseman, a small man with a
pock-marked face, here broke in, "seein' that he was a comin' from
th' diggin's an' was supposed tew have considerable gold-dust
with him, we makes bold tew stop you ladies tew ask about him,
jest as my pardner says, thinkin' you might have seen him." "We
was   sum harm had come tew him. "Sumone got him for his
gold, jest as he was   they would. "Trampas," said the Virginian,
"I thought yu'd be   to try it on me." "I'm   to be alone!"
"I'm   ." "I'm   ! I'm   !

waterbound

From Red River north and all along was herd after herd   by
high water in the rivers. Here was another herd   , and the
boss-man was as important as a hen with one chicker.. Nothing
daunted, we made our usual drive; and when the herd camped that
night, Flood, after scouting ahead to the river, returned with the
word that the Brazos had been unfordable for over a week, five
herds being   . Then all the grazing for several miles about
the crossing was already taken by the   herds, and to crowd
up and trespass on range already occupied would have been a
violation of an unwritten law. Our foreman had conceived the
scheme of getting past these   herds, if possible, which would
give us a clear field until the next large watercourse was reached.
Flood's intention was to parallel the old trail until near the river,
when, if its stage of water was not fordable, we would again seek
a lower crossing in the hope of avoiding any   herds on that
watercourse. We concluded that the "Running W" herd had turned
back, as Straw brought the report that some herd had recrossed
Red River the day before his arrival, giving for reasons the wet
season and the danger of getting   . Flood knew the foreman,
Wade Scholar, who reported having been   over a week
already with no prospect of crossing without swimming. Once
we were   for three days, severe drifts from storms at night
were experienced, delaying our progress, and we did not reach
Abilene until June 15. The grass was well forward when both herds
started, but on arriving at Red River no less than half a dozen herds
were   , one of which was George Edwards's. I took the lead
thereafter, the second herd half a day to the rear, with the almost
weekly incident of being   by intervening rivers. "   ,
your foot!   , your grandmother! From Red River north and
all along was herd after herd   by high water in the rivers.

whitewashed

He had come to Albuquerque for his lungs' sake a few years ago, and he still thrilled at the sight of bright-shawled Pueblo Indians padding along the pavements in their moccasins and queer leggings that looked like joints   of stove-pipe; while to ride in an automobile out to Isleta, which is a terribly realistic Indian village of adobe huts, made the blood beat in his temples and his fingers tremble upon his knees. But his idea of luxury is sitting down in the kitchen to a real meal of beans and biscuits and all the known varieties of jam and those horrible store   cookies and having the noise of the phonograph drowned every five minutes by a passing street car. He went out into a wide,   , high-ceiled corridor, and from that into an immense room which, but for pool tables, bar, benches, would have been like a courtyard. Farther down the main thoroughfare were several weather-boarded   stores. Nels was rubbing her hands, calling to her. She saw a house with clean   wall and brown-tiled roof. The room Shefford entered was large, with logs smoldering in a huge open fireplace, blankets covering every foot of floor space, and Indian baskets and silver ornaments everywhere, and strange Indian designs painted upon   the walls. Here were situated several edifices, the most prominent of which was a church built of wood,   , and remarkable, according to Withers, for the fact that not a nail had been used in its construction. It was kept scrupulously clean and   . A   wall enclosed a court containing another adobe building, baked with the solar beams of many summers. It was a rudely built oval amphitheater, with crumbling,   adobe walls, and roofed only over portions of the gallery reserved for the provincial "notables," but now occupied by a few shopkeepers and their wives, with a sprinkling of American travelers and ranchmen. Somehow, when she looks at a fellow, he feels like a   ." "You can be very splendid when you want to give a man that   feeling; he isn't right sure whether he's on the map or not," reproached the train-robber.

MALEEA ACKER ❧

The Inheritors

I am travelling through the mountains
on my way to ask for money from the inheritors.
Descendants of those who dug up the earth, enfolded men in mines
and broke our unions. It is warm,
a little cloudy. I am barefoot in the old car. One after another
the workers' towns, named as a try at belonging,
who thought to stop, with a tag, the old world's
bad bread and bricks through windows—here
        is the new land, where names mean nothing,
everything. Shifts of mountains frame the highway,
not growing but slowly wearing down. One shale shard
skids off the sloped abutment, sinking
to a nest of leaf just forged,
old carrot lacing out of the ground.
                A comfortable heat
nudges the car window. A new diplomat, I rehearse
for the Boards and their coffers, veiled in the distance.
                  Long were we searching, through years
of black milk, until arrival in a city
where a woman crowned, holding fire in her fist
proclaimed us free. From Vilnius also sailed
the ancestors of Jonathan, who imagined more gold
in the name *Buenos Aires*; his sailed south, ours
stayed north. A century later, we chanced to meet
there—his apartment of one window, his wife and child
slipping food from the kitchen, while the Spanish
words for the body curtained around us.
                  The Bow Valley gives way
to the last climb before sinking
into the plain. The air yellows. Soon,
the first housing development.
      My grandfather was fired
six months from his pension, from the Los Angeles missile factory,
the machines' beats shaking the floors
as he walked in for the last time, then stuttered
to a late career in movies, making sets, hammering
trees to the imaginary lakeshore, while the stars
            rode by on their horses.

At eleven, my father was screen tested;
in photographs, flawless, a welling optimist—
my grandmother would not let him go.
To be a star was to misuse the names,
to forget who has not enough. But who does
                                    not know the pleasure
of arriving in a new city, the language
unknown and every corner exchange,
every call tossed down from a tenement
so secret and glory-filled. Dust stretches
                                    in a brown haze
as I clear the foothills and fly
into the opulent plains. Lens clouds appear
on the horizon; the storm season is about to begin.
I do not know if I cannot remember
or never knew the names of my great-uncles,
the ones who stayed in Russia,
and married, and fathered children, and then
were overtaken by a cloud of ash.
                        At the airport, everyone is friendly.
I clear security. I wait in the pod
that the United States has made in this country,
and practice asking for a little more.
I picture a sphere, floating. I imagine
                              we are rising up,
and west, as the plane will.
I imagine we do not know when
we will land, or what fortune we will find,
in what language it will be shouted or
spoken, or what each name will mean.

Shotpouch

Odysseus tramps up the dusk hill, the blooming on all sides
as his mind lays down its same routine.
Song sparrow an occasional startle out of something bodied and musty,
as though having made love in the afternoon and then climbed
to the lookout without washing. Crouching to watch the sun
fold the world and there's the scent, not unpleasant,
but not like being alone. Or perhaps like being more alone than ever.
The firs wash to orange. He's pretty sure, in this version,
there's no Penelope to go back to. No wind in weeks and the rain
drops straight onto metal and woods with its one long one long
note of sorrow. Laughing at the idea of desire as anything that could quench
or be quelled. There's a bracken fern declaring at his feet.
He can't eat it, it's not a fiddlehead, though it has that same spiral of could-be-joy.
The oxalis makes him ill. And the dead mouse by the piano
made the wood floor look like obstinate hospitality.
He throws another rock over the cliff. Aeolus tosses it back,
along with the bleat of tree frogs, the shuffle of a forest finding its chair.
He shifts to unkink his legs, his heavy lidded eyes like oxen in their stalls
lowering themselves, kneeling on their fore knuckles,
letting the stiff boards and the soft manure sift between each hair.
Even when we know, he thinks, we usually have it wrong.

marina marigo wind

That it knows why halyards are made. That it lives
to make a boiling ribbon of the mast.

That it tenses spring line and aft in
endless combinations,

dreaming the hull through the arc
of its leash. Small bones of the tug;

ticker wheel of the release;
voiced only by its intimates—

sometimes, to know the world,
we must build something,

must be in the way. Because of us,
the beautiful doors opening inch by inch.

HOPETON (HOPE) ANDERSON ☙

Family Portrait

1

for Caleb (my grandson)

We all begin like you
Not by a bird
But seed and renewed promise

Of wings, then again
Sometimes the truth
Of us, composed as awkward memory

I too, saw the moo moos
In the green, green pasture
Contagiously contented

On the hill,
Where the gravel road
Separated unattended fields

From which Grandpa John's
Unlettered sermons rang
Loud through bamboo fronds

Or the moo goo gai pan
Shared with your father when small
O that town hermetically
Known as Muffin Land.

2

for Luseadra (my daughter)

You may hear it said Muffin Land
Is unlike Gotham or Captain Morgan's porch
Even the land of miraculous flowers

Or any place this side of Eden;
Not because of quaint lilts
Nor imperceptible echoes of Lilliput

But if my heart was then found
Bear woman could have stolen
Its red moon glow

And tossed it high
Into the thick topped
World of grey misty fir

And Alice, our princess child
Would have made her home
In their verdant willows

Falling like the shimmering curls
Of her bear cub hair
Which draped her shoulders
Like refracting glass or many colored quilt.

3

for Linneth (my mother)

I watch my mother now, more quiet than usual
Hating the chatter of other old women
And know she would have loved childhood
In Muffin Land, the silence and the mist

Hovering over the somber Pacific, a painter's brush
Forms glistening waters out of nothing
Common work mothers often do.

A glint of undiminished dreams
Rests in eyes where her God must reside
And memories, thick molasses
Trapped in fearful gloom

The approaching dusk, an obedient rhythm
Taps the hope of all, even the spirited child
Whose dulcet strokes broke swollen waves

Or the one who promised to master the game
Not just the crack of the bat, to interrupt her rest
But make the islands one great nation
Now restrained by wordless gloaming.

from "**Adventures**"

5

My father reminds me of me or vice versa
I thought, imagining him standing in the mist
Of Muffin Land, had he qualified for passage

When he was not old and his legs stroked
Waves, rippling nearly fixing the distance
Of those impossible shores

Though there are no muscular trunked
Almond trees, nor robust branches
There, to overhang cool cool rivers

The mind finds rest
In the blue light streaming
Out of unfamiliar harbor

Like his limp arm, featherless wing
Present on my too tiring shoulder
We descend each stair, carefully

To the emptying streets
As traffic quiets, behind us
The drawbridge closes, the hour
Too late, even for much talk.

8

for Sonianna

Without glitter of snow, winter persists
Delays necessary sun that echoes
Sweet rhythm, resonance of your name

And marine dreams born with you
Beloved, sailing the tragic Niger, the tireless Ganges
Even down the restless Ocho Rios
Passing tourists at Oracabessa

I wonder is there time
Enough time in a Sabbath's walk

To become familiar with a brook or stream
In Muffin Land
Unwind each ripple's secret shame
Or disappointment

To know the source of the green pine needles
Gathering darkly from some ancestral place
A melancholy wave, as they descend
Pour into an alien river.

JOANNE ARNOTT ✒

Sea Change

> *Poets by nature challenge death*
> —John Asfour

death is a kind of silence
slowly overtaking us, the distance
never breached, the hopes
slowly eased out of view, or snapped
startling

passion flowing rhythmic
warm heat of cohabitation
you in me
me in you
the cradling of the other in
the vast holds

silence is a kind of death
slowly overtaking us, the chatter
never slowed, the words
rarely faltering, the plans
strictly limited
improvisational

Down from the Waist

Down from the waist they're centaurs,
Though women all above
—Shakespeare

soft down and central, soft hair soft pre-feathering girdle
spontaneously erupted organic all natural ecological ergonomic
elder sister to the skirt the shirt the apron the swathe of night-clothes
younger sister to al buraq to centaurine
down from the waist of the female of the species
precious substance best scented in locus in situ
below the song and spates of milk above the precious knee and sole
down from the waist tender
down from the waist enflamed
down from the waist held soft in palm of hand

halfling bear (eclipse)

the trophy hunter has it
the scientists & the media
celebrate, debate, discuss
photos of the corpse fly
all around the world
& linger for years

the miracle of courtship
alignment sought & found
the passing of a honeymoon
the wonder of apparent difference
transcended with pleasure

the private rendezvous of
polar bear & grizzly, followed
by months of solitary gestation
of nurturing, nursing
feeding
teaching the young

all the years of a young bear's life
discoveries, missteps, accomplishments
the cultural patterning inhabited, as
taught by the mother
& the world met, step by step

all these
disappear

into bloodlust & big money
dna proofs & a too small sample
the death of a halfling bear reveals
the minds of scientific observers
& all forms of prejudice: miscegenation
still, so scandalous

this is not a freakshow
but evidence of life unfolding
& showing its shape as it goes
the elders say, *usually they fight*
but not this time

an impressive array

our bodies are our selves, only
the feints of culture can obscure it
our bodies are the repositories of
every sense impression gathered
through a lifetime, or perhaps
many lifetimes, our bodies
are ourselves, rising up
from potential to real, our bodies
are the mark of our passing, our bodies
are the soft earth of self and the panoply
of thought streams and disruptions, the
culture-tangled nots and knots and naughts
our bodies are the ground of our beings, and
the playing fields of our minds, our bodies
are what we are good at, and unconscious of,
and what we are excited with, and thoughtful
through, our bodies arrived in the world
in order for us to drink beauty through every pore
and in order for us to express beauty
as an expression of the world itself, we are
a song the world enjoys singing to itself
we do not have our bodies
any more than the world has us
a moment of self-possession passes
in the same way as does everything else

GREG BEM ✒

from **Field Notes (July–August 2014)**

What of this heat we have heard of and how to keep its thorough feelings
     alive,
Canyons as long as wide old as cannons or seers releasing the sun each
     day,
Prickling feelings being those that sit with the strange, alien grasses,
And the occasional bunch and bundle of cacti ready to become an
     obstacle.
Finally there is a layer of sweat smeared in patterns, language of work and
     effort as we move along a landscape of brown, red, and light green.

Legs discarded by the miles we trekked,
I am too distracted and burn my hand lifting my shoes from the fire,
Which, left there too long to dry, melted quite thoroughly.
Fuck, I shout, liquid plastics and fabrics attached to my hand,
My soul doing a dance before the flames, my mind thinking abruptly about
     the lack of sex in the platonic cave.

I melted my shoes.
Were good, expensive Merrills.
Gross plastic finish.

Freedom is the town of Gunnison sleeping lazily in its Utah Valley,
Many shadows of many vast mountains providing adequate layers of an
     unshackling suffocation,
And the adjacent penitentiary is larger than the town's commercial
     downtown district,
And the local Ford dealership is called Freedom Ford,
And my eyes frost over from the liberation of my car's blasting a/c as I
     imagine blowing Gunnison a kiss goodbye.

I must have left a poem in those deep valleys and canyons,
Utah racing like a heart and we are gasping for breath,
Sudden height becoming all apparent,
Including the near-ten-k elevation and its effects,
Including the breathless act of creating art in the mountains

Bring back the Browns a blanket you left wrapped up your own personal
  present from years ago,
Discovery as juvenile as adult despite the mishaps and malignment,
They are waiting like the predictions within a tapestry of ghosts,
Rubble and ruin pressed forward and getting caught in the cracks of the
  road, and all its automobiles,
And all brave automobiles travel through bravely despite the risks of the
  knowledge of the core.

The hills have been waiting,
The needle poised to strike,
And there is a rush to the waves,
Our body compressed by pebbles,
The daylight extending on and on before the final departure.

ALEX O. BLEECKER ✒

from **Responding to Neruda**

xi

Firefly vodka on the rocks
with a shot of lightning bolt
is a popular late spring cocktail.
Drinkers envision themselves
sipping, all wickered out
on wraparound porches.
The day's currency devalues
as the sun wanes. By mid-fall
a bill is a crumbling note
worth no more
than the weathered parch
it's printed on, its oilskin eaten
by all the august digits
that have fingered it.

xiv

Thursday is a fertile storm.
Women looking to conceive convince
their husbands to knock them up
at the earliest crack of thunder.
Friday is an old wives' tale
about a pregnant goddess
who regrets her ill-chosen lover.
Not what he seemed, she bit
into a ruby instead
of a pomegranate seed.

xviii

Before the war a paddy was a happy place
to grow rice. A flooded tract of arable land
manicured and angular as a Mondrian
where farmers in bamboo sedge hats
and rolled-up pant legs
got to harvesting. It was greener

than a war machine. Then some dark suits
met in a round room
and decided to manifest
a marriage. They swore an oath, Kissingered
in secret, and got to work on Project
Hell on Earth. They Pollocked napalm
across the Indochine canvas
until every seed bled yellow
under an orange cloud cluster.

xxvi

It's another syrupy cloudless day
in the South. The magnolias
have all come out,
and the sweet-toothed senator
with a taste for saccharine rhetoric
is stumping. He loves giving
speeches about nothing
being broken. They've won him
seven straight terms in the castle.
Today, though, is a special
Valentine's Day. You descend
from a storm cloud with a black
eagle patch pinned to your shoulder.
You've stolen Cupid's little bow,
and before the standing ovation
is over, you'll assassinate
a red velvet cupcake.

xxxiv

In '69 Virginia officially became
for lovers. The Blue Ridge Mountains
were dyed pink, and the Mother of Presidents
let the yippies drink her warm green
Confederate milk. Still,
every October 9th the CIA celebrates
Che's execution. Langley g-men strip down
and dance around his brick-brown heart
to panflutes and bombo drums.

Even today, under their navy-gray
virtuous suits, they're livid,
but the music doesn't feel
like it used to.

xl

Without an olive branch in its beak
a dove is just another pigeon
deemed dirty. Darwin knew their differences
were nil—they came from the same clade—
but since the English changed
the nomenclature, we judge one
a peaceful messenger, the other
a mucky plague. The coat that keeps
me warm today is the one I almost
gave away last week. Sometimes
I'm a sheep in wool clothing, other times
I'm a person disguised as a mannequin.
You're welcome to join my filthy
Christmas window display.

xlii

There's more to waiting on the Lord
than just waiting. The evangelical takes
active steps up a tortuous cliff
until a slick leaf falls from above
and he slips into a leap
of crazy faith. The dude believes
it's better to abide and lose
than to never even try
for a strike. Easy to say
when you're poolside sipping margaritas
in a lime green leisure suit
with *Jesus* stitched to the chest,
but don't stand on top of a hill
holding a golf club over your head
unless it's a 2-iron. Even God
doesn't like hitting
with a 2-iron.

YVONNE BLOMER ☙

In the Box from the World Wildlife Fund
(a curtal sonnet)

there is the last Polar Bear.
In the belly of the box, the bear's
hollow high-strung heart
rhythmed in plush down,
a stroke of a black frown
for what melts and what is dead.

The boy's blonde-shod head
hangs off his bed. He sleeps and snores,
his toes curl, his fingers slacken straight.
The boy, his skin white under the lantern
                    of Ursa's light.

Blood Letting

If a tourniquet
the vein's pinch an accusation.
If untoned muscle.

If I help
the nurse's eyes deep and
my marbled blood.

When my son
the vein slides away. If
pain, don't flinch.

When it's me
the colour drains from husband
if he watches.

If water, blood.
If chocolate on tongue, syrup.
If I walk all day.

If the doctor calls.
If I run for the phone.
All night, sweats.

First Sunset

for RG

The celestial glow of orange.
Strange light of what's forgotten lines your face.

From the ferry: peaks and blue smoke along the island's hills.
We stand, distant and blue; the ferry peaks on the hills of tide.

What if pregnant, I ask, your whiskers grey?
Or merely grey in this whiskered dusk.

The hour of distortions, refracted light.
I deflect tenderness, your hand on my hip.

Each pause from crimson to black sky, an empty house.
Each empty house a lee shore.

Sunset, you say, and sex. Dogs howl as dusk comes on.
What is natural, I say, meaning fog or low cloud on a hillside.

Smoke, you say, lit by dogs.
Dogs, I say, hackles at the door. Death I say.

When the sun's light dies, Azimuth, I say.
You nod, thinking, star.

I turn away.

A Walk in Mushrooms

If decay.
If I had a hat shaped just like that, or a smile.
If my ribs folded together.
If like coral glowing in the damp of sea leaves.
If a boy with blue eyes mushrooms in.
If he doesn't.
If slick as slug trails, yellow snow, brain fungus.
If decaying meant fog on the ground, fog between the needles and pines.
If I would get my scarf to scoop my neck like curly haired elf cup.
If walking, if leaning in like two booted amanita.
If walking I walked right out of my runners.
If doubled, coupled, maroon red.
If I lived here, spores.

DENNIS E. BOLEN ☙

Everybody

Everybody knew somebody

>   Age of battered pickup
>   cigarette load ashtray butt

Everybody knew

>   grease coif armpit stain
>   snagglepick match tooth

>   Beyond
only the responsibly parented survive...

Everybody knew beltless toddler

Everybody

>   Unrestrain seat bench projectile
>   to the outskirts of wisdom

>   Everybody knew somebody dead
>   of car wreck

>   Undershirt men
>   cross-eye sway fatigue
>   pace toward a next shift
>   to hew and draw and maintain
>   skirted metal house with wheels
>   rented concrete

>   Smoke death and like it

everybody knew

>   to cull those lucky not otherwise demised
>   of proud ignorance

Everybody knew

    none should crave education
    Drop out by 16 or you're not a man

Everybody knew

    alcoholic
    frown drink burp asleep
    door-slam solitary

Everybody knew men curse pregnant women

Weep
Shout
Things broken

        When the truck flies everybody off the road
        swat the kid who won't shut up
        fiddle the dial radio
        Leaden sad song
        soon silence

Greenchain Canticle

Out aside the tarmac
under breezeway shingles huff
shoulder men to shoulder
Those whom fate determines
suffer the splinter
bruise
     of forestry
     rash abrasion
     ragged cut

          Twenty stations haul six grades each
          Fresh hewn fir and poison cedar
          cast-iron hemlock
          lead log vengeful
          at the affront of being sawn

I scarce had arms 'til the summer of '73
     wing rough every sodden stick
     jagged stacks
feed the hunter wheel-legged carry machine

     Alberni Pacific Division
     longest greenchain extant still
     in all the then lumbering world

First shift nightmare by lunch break
drive home barely bear press of
     clutch pedal to foot

          And that gnawing knowing
          before rest could help anything
          back again to the dreadful wood river
          streaming as never to stop

     the crush

     tensile authoritative structural beams
     to make lurchmen dream of ease

to fade a summer afternoon
more than a beer after the shift
Escape so far
deep

from   hurtful heat
                 back crack

      Fatigue so drunken

      Horror of wet two-by-six
            twenty-foot heft
            swarm in sodden clutter

      But the grain was clear
      and the tooth rig shrieked
      delight at blade rip

into pure tree-flesh
Effusion of diamond fleck
      wet confetti
           about the world

      of us millers deaf

      to the outside pleasance
            of poised time
            Champagne with fish roe
            Mountain view and sea
            Pleasing shape
            to put one's hand to

            We are
with callus and leather apron
resin souls
amid true boards travelling

Barred by endless log cabinetry
forgotten in dented truck

mortgaged sport coupe
Who through dullness perpetuate
the exiled mind
leaked youth and financed future
4pm pickup tailgate
parking lot tankcar drink
littered ditch glass
lakeside roadway side-glitter
to commemorate passenger girlfriend
of the millionth drop-out conscript

Whose thick dirty digits
in a yearn dizzy
sneak beneath feminine waistband
and by shortness of sight nightly swear
life-long fealty to the chain
running for the builders
proud constructors
hammerists

Conveyor mother mechanical

AMARANTH BORSUK ☙

Shifting Shapes

1. Some Magicians Are like Sculptors

Pinwheel, you are a talisman guiding the light of astral bodies: save it up and blast the bad rays back to space. Backspace. Back up. You cultivate a telic chakra in your cyclone of bicycle spokes (that's only when your momentum's arrested, otherwise you move quick as culture and no one can see you). Stilled, one might mistake you for a gorgeous gorget (go-getter) circling the neck of a cloud, but in fact you are sharp, you cut low, low cut, your design a palindrome: read all the way round, you return to moraled pin. Your sound: mylar streamers in blossoming cherry while crop dusters drift silently across bucolic palimpsests of field. Or no, it looks like someone's left the sound off. *If the game won't start*, you say, *try blowing on the cartridge.*

2. Some Clothes Are like Magic

You are a nautilus shell. Turned in on yourself (never navel-gazing), as you move, sliding footwise over slate, your palletted shell clicks, a walking mosaic, clattering, yet put together. You are palpable—all eyes upon you, a noise like the syncopated pop of an expandable straw escapes. Or maybe a ream of scrap paper slipping, sheet by sheet, from a desk. *No, a cascade of hot milk through latte's foam*, you think and gasp, distracted by the compact skin of flags through which you semaphore your intent: to pack and unpack your suitcase to grand effect. Each fold invites its opposite in this slow performance of self fashioning. When you finally open up, all that's left is a voice on a radio tuned to static: *over and out.*

3. Some Shapes Are like Not Being Worn

You arrive pressed carefully in a sealed bag that opens with a sigh, labeled J. Crew. J/K, you hate preppy chic, but like shrink-wrapped catalogue-wear (it's true) your creases will never come out. Your design bug is a feature: pentagram folds for keeps provide a restrained anarchy. Your bright song, a holiday tune: "Silver Belle." At the phrase *Roll out!* you transform from a Christmas star to an angel's red carpet look (still the tops), a pleated pouf that magnifies her mecha shape. Your sound is neon's buzz, radiating a power pose, no one sees you close your five fabric fingers into a fist. Say it: *easy mockery.* No one messes with you, Missy, when you un-origami and pump up the volume on your shiny Michelin suit to step into the night.

Show of Hands

1. a bird in the
2. a dab
3. a firm
4. a free
5. a helping
6. a swift
7. an old
8. at the   of
9. back
10. bound   and foot
11. by
12. by his own
13. by the   of
14. cap in
15. climbed   over
16. close at
17. cold   warm heart
18. first
19. from   to
20. got her   dirty
21. got his   in it
22. forced his
23.   back
24.   down
25.   full
26.   in
27.   in glove
28.   in
29.   me down
30.   off
31.   on deck
32.   on heart
33.   on the plow
34.   out
35.   over

36.   to mouth
37.   tied
38.   up
39. hat in
40. hold
41. idle
42. in good
43. in the palm of his
44. into his own
45. lay a   on
46. lend a
47. lift   against
48. like the back of her
49. many
50. near to
51. on
52. on one
53. on the other
54. out of
55. played into their
56. sat on his
57. second
58. shook
59. sleight of
60. the upper
61. the whip
62. threw his   up
63. try one's
64. upper
65. wait on   and foot
66. washed his   of it
67. well in
68. with a warm
69. with one   tied behind her back
70. with her own fair
71. wringing their

GEORGE BOWERING ✎

Canadian Life

Canadian life goes on. Trucks in the back alley
groan the way my cousin groaned when they finally
lifted the heavy machine off him. It's a national
question we are too busy to answer, holes appear
and we patch them with pavement, then more
holes appear, lines get longer at the credit union,
Canadian life goes on, sunlight caught in newspapers,
no question about it, Toronto really *is* interesting.

My cousin died anyway, not making the news, not
able to see his mother again, the traffic returned
to speed, I noticed a new hesitation in my father's walk.
My face is getting old faster than the sky is, Canadian
skies are among our favourite, as for example the sky
over southern Manitoba when you are twenty years old
and your moustache is coming in, the moustache that
surprised you by going white some years later, but

Canadian life goes on in the Big White, poetry seeps
into the prairies, my father chased my mother
through the kitchen, reading *Venus and Adonis* to her.
A lot of things are louder than Shakespeare, but now
we have mute buttons on everything, including boyfriends
with eyes for your car, soccer fans in the street,
Nova Scotia too far past the horizon to fret your
brow. I'll take a pill for Canadian life, and watch it
from the upstairs bedroom window, dear friends.

Curiosity

The neonate looked up at me with eyes
I have known forever. Then clouds, white on top,
grey underneath, slid behind those eyes, the way
a dog methodically licks vanilla ice cream
out of a paper cup. I step all over images
people have left behind in their hurry
to get to the delicatessen, where a famous
admiral is sitting down to a heavy sandwich.
His eyes have seen dark clouds in a medicine chest,
dancing men on a moist deck; he eats with
decorum, his devotees at the window, hands
beside their eyes, hungry and midsize in their
spring outfits. The baby knew I was there,
I know this for a certainty, its placid demeanor
no match for my anxiety, the quality
that has got me through a thousand confrontations.
If you have any desire to know my secret heart,
read on, I hear it coming, we can divine
the cosmic weather's intentions by its ability
to imitate the peace beyond curiosity.

Father's Day

Trembling stalactites are an omen if you like—
a presentiment of something unknown is to be
expected. But are you likely to see any, likely
to hear their music? Dance with me, Henry. Not
as I heard this morning the 1953 music of Betty
Roché, and in this time of the easily awesome,
isn't that something?
                      I've been in favour of
something all my life, even shepherd's thumb
is something. There will be plenty of time
for the absence of something, and did we not
hear the silent drop of a hammerhead on that note?
I'm older than the boy in 1953, who knew there was
a world no neighbourhood had even stopped to give
a song about. So when Billy Eckstine was faking it,
it was still it, a something you needn't even
ask your father about, your father you loved,
and who told you how to remember which were
stalactites, who spent his time in science and
let you handle fiction. He showed you how to
hold a hammer at the top end, a lesson about
fulcrum, one supposes. If he believed in omens
you never heard about it. If he only got to read about
things you would later go and see, well, they
ought to name a day for such a person.

Hard Under, High Above

Once in a while you bite your tongue
or a rock goes down the hillside wrong,

the earth itself tips not quite right
and nobody notices, but you notice;

your sister ought to notice but she's
watching ancient game shows on TV.

Your sister and you have the same scabs
on the same portions of your lower limbs

but she will never stand on a stage and
exhibit them for a slim public regard

though she is slim herself, what you'd call
witchy gaunt, came years ago sliding

out the birth canal you'd made your
rough way. Once in a while you bite your

knuckle in a blend of fear and regret,
or sudden newts want to cross the road

unattended by sound of any kind,
those purblind sojourners, poor rubber

tongues crawling over the macadam
between somewhere and somewhere else

for no reason perceivable by this driver
intent on the curvature of the earth

or his spine while he stands on two feet
puzzled by his ability, biting the bullet.

Myth is History

The toilet paper I've used during my life—
do I owe the earth a tree? Two trees?
But wait, haven't my turds fed the earth,
or were they slid into the Sea?

At the University of California someone said
we western civilization people have cut off nature,
returning our fertile product not to the earth
but into the ocean, where all the salt is, except
that in the peanut butter I bought today, a jar
otherwise free of additives. Think about salt
in your stomach, in your small intestine, think about
those Road movies, Crosby and Hope back to that sound stage
where extras keep putting on ruffled sleeves and moustaches,
their fecal discharge in the Bay, not leaking nutrients
into a sun-warmed pasture. Southern California poetry
too could use some advice from was it Kantorowicz?
He said drop that basketball, pick up a hoe, and even your life.

Olde Valley Guy's Plaint

Was it scenery or furniture? I mean the
forest, alright, sparse trees on the hillside,
the lake covering something this generation
knew nothing about, the rocks spilled into
deltas now lichened. I guess the answer depends
on whether you are a citizen or a god
among others.

                    Speaking of the lake and such,
how many times have I leaned over our rail,
biting a peach we brought down from
my home town?

[long pause]

Is this furniture, a notation by Death,
my acquaintance of long standing in dark grey,
or disbelief, scenery I greeted daily as earth's
unclarified demeanor?

                    Need everything now
be so obdurate for us citizens, obdurate
and never noticed by the gods we plead
our quiet cases to?

The Maltese M

Surely it tells us something that more people
read *Paradise Lost* than even begin reading *Paradise
Regained.* Things used to be different, but now
more people say "Oh, Hell!" than say "Heavens
to Betsy!" Of course a lot of those nice old names
have fallen into disuse, like spats or sugar tongs.
I was thinking of reading some more Milton because
his name starts with M, as does Marlowe,
whom I am reading now after a long hiatus.
Have you ever noticed that hiati are getting
longer these days? And really, there isn't one,
not a true one, because I didn't read Marlowe
so much as be the kind of person who has
read Marlowe, who went sometimes as Merlin,
as does the wise wife of my longtime friend Dave
McFadden, whose books of poetry I have been reading
for all our adult lives. Dave believes that Paradise
is here right now, all around us, and so he
absorbs it and bears witness that life is not
all subway noise and undersalted eggs. Heavens
to Betsy, I say to him, more people confess
willingly to reading your books of poetry than
even know about *Paradise Regained* in any edition.
He smiles like a bodhisattva who will have
no specific religion until time leaks out under the door.

JULES BOYKOFF ☙

Silent Sting

*

So much depends
          on the buzz of the bee
                  the flap of a wing
      the click of the keys
                        while so much bends
         with the sophistry I sell
               myself festooned and jaunty
    a rumpus   a curio   a theory
               a groundswell of sorts

*

grasshopping from topic to topic
               objects in mirror appear
      larger than our present imperfect
     furious blur of grammar
                another white boy with a fat bag
        of theory
    another cache drive-by
           mowing the hopelessly unfashionable
      the strange
          grasshopper its coloration
    ablaze with protoplasm
      the past pressing predictions
     into commemorative coins you
yellowfinch flitting by the river
       with your economics and thistled breath

*

skullduggery   toxicology   tiny hopper   asset bubble

*

careening from issue to issue
                              event to event
                                          limb to limb
to hurtle: an asset bubble of sorts

                              we made it appear
            to disappear
                    the bees the birds
            and the keyboards too

                    *

hopping on command
                        not ushered
                                but coaxed

KATE BRAID ✎

Pines in May
  (painted by Emily Carr)

Dancing.
Did you ever see a tree
dancing? She did.
Young ones at the front,
adolescents behind,
a mother over all
towering out of sight.
But the great
grandmother of everything
is sky.

Whenever she gives us sky
it is a blue gift of grace
making all the rest possible.

Pine trees frisk in great
spirals whose goal is always
upward,
pine trees dancing in May,
a private party
and Emily one of the few
who could read the invitation.
There will be dancing,
it would say
written on cedar and fir and pine
in an envelope of deep black dirt.

Untitled

(painted by Emily Carr)

Creatures peer out from everywhere.
They see everything with those eyes.

In the darkness
of earth rising,
only trees reveal themselves
open as organ pipes in some hymn
that leaves me trembling.

These trees live without me.

After they are gone, houses
will take their place but spirits
will linger here. Ghosts will
wander up the stairwell
of some child's dreams.
The child will wake with a cry
not sure if it's fear
or awe

something about organ music
something about animals everywhere
with eyes. Something about eyes.

Old and New Forest

(painted by Emily Carr)

Welcome to the house of giants, dozens
of evergreens and a host of babies at their feet.
Picture it as a family photograph in a wood
frame coloured in tones of romance and regret.

Being somewhat related, we keep it on the mantle.
Unaware of its presence most of the time, taking it
for granted along with other family
photographs of matriarchs, patriarchs,
kids who grew old when we weren't looking.

We dust it off, show it only when visitors appear.
This was ours, we say, and are admired
for what? For claiming ownership? Neglect?

Later, when the guests are gone, Mother
feels uncomfortable, runs a finger
over the pale glass.

Remember? she asks vaguely.
Father stirs in his easy chair.
Remember those forests?
Something in her wants to weep.

BILL CARTY

Kiko Is Missing

But her picture is
everywhere and her
owner, my neighbor, paces
the living room talking
to the tessellations
of her carpet but not
to Kiko, who is missing.

My grandmother spoke
to patterns too,
she refused to look up from
the museum's marble
tiles to the sculptures.
She said, "My niece
writes wonderful poems,"

but she had no niece
and hardly had me
in mind. She said,
"I am no longer
the person who once
tried everything."

Then she gave me
my grandfather's axe.
I replaced the head,
and I replaced the handle.
It is my axe now.

Ocean, the Great Conductor

For about thirty seconds the plane
was the brightest planet,
so directly were we in its path.

The interior of the car was esophageal red,
and in the headlights, my dancing
a reenactment of my deep shame of dancing.

We had no governor, only the moon
making a smaller moon
on the car hood.

There were no waves, only a tension
at the surface, a humming
like the bell with a bee's nest for a clapper.

ALLISON COBB ❧

Look

Oh be
hilarious, oh spill
yourself into the general dis
-course, Smurf
mushroom house I hated
before I even opened the Christmas box—all
those creepy blue men in my bedroom. But I pretended
to love them suckled as I was on the code of being female—don't hurt
their famous feelings above all—be dead
before ugly, improper—it means
false, what doesn't fit: My whole skin every cell and synapse every breath
and bit of nourishment leaked to me from womb onward came
courtesy of your shining
tax dollars and our movie
star president's love for Star
Wars—the missile
not the movie. *Lost*
Almost he called it, my father, a joke: Los
Alamos, the cottonwoods, a tree that means
water in the desert you can live there. Lost
Almost it was
his joke it always came
out of his mouth first, we learned everything
out of that mouth—my mother, I had her
body at twelve held
his hand and pretended I owned him
as husband, could I look
old enough for that—could I hold that kind of
superpower? Rage. I didn't understand then
how it could blank one—a woman
much later asking if I worried about getting sick being from there I
couldn't answer I'd never thought of it I didn't know any sick people
who could be me I hated
that woman for her question my dis
-ease, I hated or really feared, we feared the Cave Woman. She lived
in the canyon between the town and the lab beneath
Omega Bridge in a cave everyone
said I never saw her but my friend's mom warned us be careful my

boyfriend drove his VW down at night to try and find her no one I
knew ever did, but USA Today reported in 2004 a man living in a cave
in Los Alamos with solar and a grow-op and a glass front door.
They charged him with possession. There is not
a real law I guess against squatting in a government-owned cave in
the richest county in the country. He pleaded not guilty. The Deputy
Fire Chief said he was impressed with the man's ability to live in such
style unseen in the zone of exclusive smurfdom sorcerers—the future
is really now remember how you exploded how the boy said nice
books I mean nice but they need tanning, the reporter said she
appreciated the animal for how it died without whining. According to
the New York [war] Times the people of the
richest county Lost Al
-most live eleven years longer, on average, than the people of the
poorest: Clay County, Kentucky. Hilarious comes from Greek for
joyous, Kentucky is Iroquois or Shawnee perhaps for meadow or a
shining river in the midst of it. Let us hang
next to Thomas Jefferson this portrait of the Sampson
Pearlymussel gone extinct in Kentucky in 1984, and the Disappeared
Island Elugelab, vaporized in Earth's first
thermonuclear fire—all part of our national ab-
cessence inside the White
Skull House of cavities for feelings. "I felt," she wrote in her portrait
book of extinct species, "like I
could be the one
to give them a voice." She counted
my breaths as I spoke
from the French: *the no*
turns out to be nothing
but a yes…the injunction to look
at what looks back—the one
the gun's still
pointed at

ALICIA COHEN ✺

Civic Life

these streets be
trued with airy tools
warm on the shoulder
the wind we swim in and with which air
we dead speak

let me tell you of my time
metal roams free full of flame
retardant plastic and leather
stenching the ear

their exhaustpipe breath burns the lungs of song
and spree on errands like speed hunting itself
if the mountain lion
were free of feeling and full of unlimitedness'
extreme extent

here the mountain lion is to be gone from the world
freeway
cars pose in mad dinosaur armature

Oregon Coast by Joyce Herbst

document of what was
inexhaustible
oyster pickers
dwarfing forest
long canoe

vast
work of recording
vast
goodbye

never to consent
at the outset nor
in the aftermath

what happened is all we have
not done

come

Tillamook Coast Forest

evidence of our unsolitary death
in piles and
fiery wisps
a hundred hundred horses and ten ten thousand mesohippuses
full of missing

being in
my old canoe

my seagreen daughter's eyes are destined to loss' fullness
I cannot hold to forever's ocean

  smoke proof
      the love of the world
the bird's held   gaze
winging past

long long to buoy
each pierced being flies

in fury suffered
at the cusp
approach of the wilderness
looking toward the city
edge of the carnage

undoing the cherished forest
Tillamook attended to
with reckless laboriousness
municipal fortune

suppression stoked
storm burns beginning in '33
forest fire so hot it storms
blare of attention's anger is deafening
and recurs like
lumber grows a logic
that turns hot

each forest branches outside the clearcut to come and
arcane
the song is wild soft

JEN COLEMAN ❧

Gossip

(after ink drawings on rice paper by Susan D'Amato)

Where can I find someone to ignore all this language
so we can really talk?
—Chuang Tzu

1)
The universe is a heavy breather
out here in the desert. So it
tells itself, so it told me
as it sighed and whispered
in the same ear the same
whisper that whispers from the ink
on your hollow ink-pushing feather.

2)
The grass as well on seeing
the ink is surprised to see its
own gesture, the poppies abashed
to see their intimacy with the wind,
the rain, its sparseness noted,
the coyote ideas howling
with the deeper need of the small flower,
tiny and abundant yellow
caught and saved as a note.

3)
Ink is unforgiving, a small liquid shadow
so soon dry. Except that it is fond:
kindness to the poppy's moment changing even
in perpetual stillness, to the grass and its various
elegances, to the single ant, the seed, fond
of the "hey" duck full of wondering at regular intervals.

4)
The cottonwood tree up over the spring
told me about writing exactly
the same poem I am writing to you now
ten thousand days ago, and, waving its leaves
like the hands of ten thousand Miss Americas,
the tree told me too that it did your paintings,
too, all of them, the done ones
and the not-yet-done ones.

That tree is an asshole.

5)
The bone told me
how it doesn't regret clinging to life,
but how only in its boneliness
is there a truly unspeakable intimacy
with light and the charcoal and ink
and the way it is like a tongue
and a palm and flesh and also pleasure
in the ways it is not like flesh. And this bone
(a sheep bone or a bone of the sea or leg or spine)
whispered to the heavy-breathing universe
the same whisper that whispers from the ink.

Playa, Summer Lake, June 2014

Aerosmith

She rather handsome, we kinda looked the same
–Tiny Bradshaw, 1951, "Train Kept A-Rollin'"
recorded by Aerosmith, on *Get Your Wings* (1974).

The soft white belly, a vicious belly, an animal
  belly, a belly fat as food for an eagle.

As a girl, I wanted to hook the bullhead from the still
dark swell under the drain pipe again and haul it out,
stroke the soft breathing belly, slip the fish back
into the dark cool, *get along, sweet little fish,*
get along, on your way.

And as a girl in the attic, belly sweating in the infinite
summer heat, I wanted to set the needle
in the same deep drum groove with flesh-air,
sweating, and think on the fresh rage shape of it.

Drain kept rolling, all night long,
drain kept rolling all night long, drain
kept rolling all night long, drain kept
a rolling all night long

Its hot in the attic and the records warp and I
sweat blood and coal because to sweat coal
is as easy as being sucked out as oil. Sometimes
as a girl you are sucked out as oil,

sometimes *in heat,* sometimes *in love*
carved out as cool wet peat
and dried in the hot sun.
Sometimes all you do is shape shift.

At the edge of the creek by the drain pipe
where I sing a wasp with a dark spot on each wing
erases words in flight, flying its weird flight

around meaning lingered. At the edge of the creek
under the sewer pipe maybe just that one bullhead
lives plus crayfish in the deep cool where as a girl
I throw down my hook to catch it again.

But I just couldn't tell her so no no no
Get along, sweet little breath-shape
 get along with my tongue, a sound-shape shifter
shifting with a lip a shaped creek

from the depths of my lungs into my well-mouth
in the rage shape of a song, get along.
And in the attic's small window where a light-creek
flows in and settles on a record spinning,

a wasp fills my window with its paper nest
of lost words, expanding with the entire reason I want
to be not a girl or an eagle,

a barracuda, demon, wasp, or man with long
long powerful legs. I never wanted
to be a girl, but I never wanted
to be anything else. Except Aerosmith

kicking the dirt outside the yard, kicking
the dog-shuffled dirt outside a dark Memphis prison.

STEPHEN COLLIS ☙

The Word

We were
Decaying already
Our throats
The problem of
The relation between
These signs taken
As these signs
Taken to mean
And make
Arbours
And orchards
Where we write
On the skins
Of apples or
Recoil from
The temptation
To understand
Our urges too well
So fuck it
This is the word
And we are unmaking
The amplitude
Of the boundaries
We do and do not
Still dwell within

The Insurgencies

We were like
The people
Meant some specific
Though difficult group
Rising meant that
Fed up with
Tally of harms
Digital wealth in some
Off-shore pirate haven
Armies moving everywhere
Planet in decline
The fierce precarity of
Just giving a shit
The people are
Having gathered
That we weren't
Going to go away
Place of assembly
Place we could organize
Place we could plan

Toussaint 2011

All our algebras
Defunct
Ghosts tread
On neurons
That shadow
Language
An opera
No one hears
Fills tents
We continue
To imagine
Long after
They are gone
On the lawns
Of galleries
A lion rising
Red and as luck
Would have it
New political
Forms emerged
Nature called
Them spectres
Scientists
Possibilities
The rest of us
Out to pick
Remnant berries
In the cool morning

The World is Never Enough With Us

I should apologize for yet another
Poem about death   and political economy
But the daily walk is the graveyard
Emily, treading, treading
Like the Fang people of Africa with the
Bundled sticks of their dead dried
Folded and packed around on their backs
Thin children that never wake or complain

*

I open a file called "no file"
A messianic cloud of media
Rising above rioting squares
The colony called "don't stop"
Does not stop—flails against futurity

It could yet be about the end of corruption
It could yet be about better worlds
It stops just outside of town, rumbling
The largest truck you've ever seen
Its bucket filled with half the earth—literally

*

The other night I read a novel
In the file called "no file" I lodge
Records of evacuations, evictions
Foreclosures and dispossessions

According to the avant-garde
This isn't new
And "new" means "maybe we can
sell you one more of these"

But I am upbeat despite the end-times
Faux comforts and police horizons

*

My daughters are shopping at the mall
It's a green space we call "eternity"
All their lives are an imaginary
Of the yet-to-come

Even the mall is still only a dry unceded field
Mice wander and developers eye
With hungry imaginations crooning

You're so fucking spatial
I wish I was spatial

*

Note to self:
Perimeters are difficult to discern
And species are in constant motion
Curling towards their disappearance
Engines culling "data" we will not read

I find it difficult
To imagine the lives of many others
Though their abandoned velour couches
Can be found in the forest
Soggy Blue Star Dust, Dr. Pepper brown

*

Mostly we keep blowing
Each other up
Like bombs are our way of saying

S'up, I'm here too
Is this crazy human meat times or what?
Now let's keep making money, death mill daddy-O

*

My daughters cannot decide:
Zombie movie or cell phones?
I could still be dreaming
Of France and revolutions
Or walking between the etched tombstones

*

I tell the girls what matters
Is the soft light just back
Of the collective's desiring eye
The beach we build beneath
The mall's unmade paving stones
(though I do not mention
the continuous rule of dead
labour over living
or their future riveting
to a single fraction of time)

We choose the Zombie movie
Because life is like that

*

Emily, shall we hide our brave face
On this daily walk
Or take us simultaneous
As complicit beings wondering
How to stop, but carry on differently—
All we're freighted with—
Unearned privilege, debt, former colonies
Muttering doges, sputtering lanterns
The metallic insides of the earth
The proximity of death squads—
And still slink silently
Towards better worlds?

*

Of course complicity just means
You have to change yourself entire
When changing the tired world

Its Molotov banquets
Its endless lines of tanks idling nearby
Its schools for unlearning indigeneity

*

As if all we had to do was
Make the world strange again, hmm?
What is the nearness
Of economies and lobotomies?
Note how money is
The cryogenic liquid
Of this period evaporating
What lasts
And filling the tanks of
Sulphurous lies—

Just don't look up at the eyedroppers
Poised above our frozen faces
As we gaze at the empyrean
Of stained acoustic ceiling tiles

*

Meanwhile beneath the glassy surfaces
Of our smartphones—deep in pocket—
Young girls and boys
My daughters' ages and younger
Pull handfuls of dusky coltan
From a muddy trench in the Congo
And somewhere some kid—god love him—
Says *it's all good*
Just before his brains become
Some zombie's next meal

Bright Paper

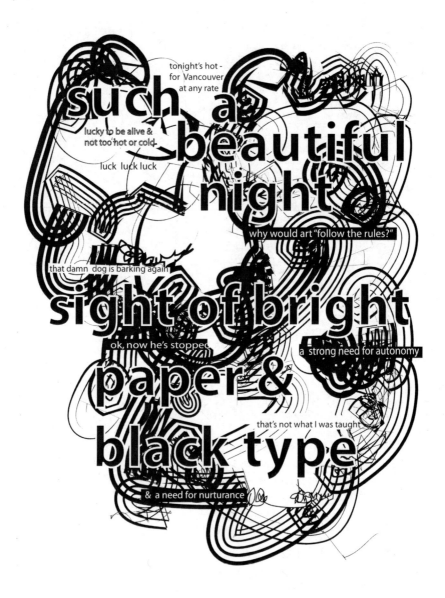

such a
beautiful
night

sight of bright
paper &
black type

tonight's hot -
for Vancouver
at any rate

lucky to be alive &
not too hot or cold

luck luck luck

why would art "follow the rules?"

that damn dog is barking again

ok, now he's stopped

a strong need for autonomy

that's not what I was taught

& a need for nurturance

Ocular Queries

why did you want to say this?

                                            why do you want to say this?

          what is worth saying?

                                                what is worth seeing?

          what is **really** worth saying??

                                                who wants to say it?

what is **really** worth seeing?

                              say/si/sigh/search/shiver

               what was being said?

                    what do you want to say?

what did they want to say

                                  how to say this?

                    how did he want to say it?

                  what should be said?

              say/see/sight/sound/aural/oral/ocular/query

PETER CULLEY ☙

Cruel Summer

(after Wallace Stevens)

He was in Nanaimo writing letters to
Marshall, every now &
then walking down to the playhouse
for a smoke. The heavy leafage
of a wet June absorbed the roar
of the highway so he sat on the damp
carpet he'd slung over the old garden
chair & picked up and put down
the book that had begun to curl
on the dusty table raising more dust.
He trades places with the cat
so that when the gravel trucks gear
down or loudly up the cat can watch them pass
& he can pretend to read.

It was almost time for Rockford
when the news intervened. Outside the last
bees on Planet Earth rubbed sagey
pollen on their undercarriages.
Noting this he raised his eyes from the
newscrawl to a copper Ford drifting
thru the twilit Bel-Air of the Ford
administration. This is the part of the sublime
from which we shrink: Sepulveda, Ventura
& Culver City are to him
an approximate haze as hard as calcium,
unspooling painkillers at every point
of the compass. Something shifts &
then he shifts. He apologises
to the dead space where he had been sleeping.

ii

He wakes in the pollarded half-shade of a dying
walnut. The half-audible early birds tweet
ear bones press against each other
a passing satellite pings its archive.

Night had been a tree to him moving through space,
sparing him memorable dreams, something
medication never quite achieved
but if you sit there thinking it goes dim
the golfball grain comes rushing in
like water through a window. All he knows
of the moon—its interlocking t-shapes
of broom yellow fanning
oilslick tailfeather—is that its
both outside & above, a bell held in a cup.

The pain is such a little thing to be wandering
abroad like that. He becomes aware of the
heavy air & that he's awake,
a hiss of decompression through the leaves
hanging heavy in a hoary-hanging sky
sickly after the rain hit, turning west
he hallucinates as it falls each ring of the tree.

iii

He hangs hangers in a
cupboard left to right

the wind chime's
soft memory gonging

across his neck,
Chico Hamilton style—

a handswidth or two
more or less, unstrapping

the braces, snapping brasses
hinged ruler with oil, rarely looking up,

even at those shivers of bleached
green leaf piercings

where other people move
through the light more or less as he does

but rarely with that quadrant over-the-shoulder-
you-see-what-he-sees angle—no

narrating parrot or hummingbird
or offshore bee would follow so close

knowing neither right nor left
nor above nor below

bouncing around
at the end of a pineal stalk

like the third eye of realism
squinting through the low cloud.

A Poem for the Seattle Poets

Blue from Player's Plain
Pharoah & Coltrane
hopped-up hummingbirds
raging on raw honey, oysters &
barnacle-scraping soul-encounters
buzz the pre-dawn Lynnwood rain

Blue from Winslow Homer
or someone with no home to go to
he wet his finger west
& traces out the weather week
his weakest hunch a sheriff's gut
thrust out for the informer

Blue Six's "Music & Wine"
was a song we heard all the time
before the macrobiotic encounter
split the silver monitor—the crashing
symptoms came complete
with waves of "Om" on yellow gull feet

Blue moon's a passenger with no ID
& nothing solid in the dictionary
no per diem, no booking fee,
no very convincing reason to be
alone in swollen solidarity with
the puffer, the skink & the manatee

CHRISTINE DEAVEL ❧

From the Ground Up

At Boren and Jefferson
The Mountain came to watch me.
It walked as I walked.
At Ninth and Jefferson
it saw me to my feet
in their shoes.
It saw the late November light
touch my head
as I walked by the hospital.

———————————————

Crows shop precisely
from a trash can.

A sorting intelligence
they share with people.

I watched a man lift out
a discarded cup.

He tipped back his head to drink,
like they do.

———————————————

Halfway up that neighborhood's immense hill
is a tiny white church.
Go around the side
to the small stoop
you'll see a flattened pile
of woody stems
and pieces of cloth.

I'm thinking
some being comes to that door
but no one goes in or out.

Halfway down.
I could have said
halfway down, too.

───────────────

The bird wing
on the sidewalk
is beautiful. O my god.

Gray and white
severed wing
on the busted cement. Shit.

Extended
the way it would be for,
you know

(I don't want to say the word
because, Jesus,
it wasn't doing that).

───────────────

On the path by the park's hedge
two juncos stepped out
and joined me on my walk,
a full measure
of tipping toward and away,
until we parted company.
Not ways, though.
I hope
we did not part ways.

SARAH DE LEEUW ✎

Copper[1] River

an extract from "Skeena"

We are on such familiar terms
locals to each other, touching
one-and-a-half million years.

Rock work   twisting radials   of ammonites.

Pressed. A sea.

You deliver to me a sea from long before we are us.

...

From *Forest Sciences Prince Rupert Forest Region: Floodplain Erosion
Hazard Mapping Zymoetz (Copper) River, Terrace, BC (August 1996)*:

In the early 1960s, the Copper River Forest Road was built. The road
followed the river for 50 kilometers and ended north of Limonite Creek.
Long sections of the road were built on the floodplain. In the early 1970s,
the natural gas pipeline from Smithers to Terrace through the Telkwa
Pass was also routed along the lower Zymoetz River. In November 1978,
a 100-year flood eroded many sections of the road and the pipeline: some
sections were abandoned, others re-built. Repeated flooding in 1988, 1991,
and 1992 damaged and eroded many of the rebuilt road sections. What had
been considered a "stable" road location for the first 15 years, now seemed
to have become a chronic and expensive problem demanding long-term
solutions.

...

Coral reefs and plankton, lace-like
hemlock bows now, now after the salt
has sunk, left pale spice in fossils

---

[1] The "Copper" River is only called The Copper River by "locals" (principally
settler locals). On maps and in most "formal" (e.g. not local but, rather, scientific
or touristic) documents and records, the river is referred to as the Zymoetz. The
Copper/Zymoetz is home to the locally famous Copper River Fossil Beds.

white crystal quartz and trace
elements, exoskeleton sketch lines.

Running red today this clay
day, episodic flooding
those beds of Jurassic
sleep stirring up your bottom
sediments, wet erosion
dust thickened into muck
stuck against the cottonwood
islands plunked in our wandering
gravel bed channels.

Braid into me flat on this earth's skin
forget temptations of aggradations
stay channel open, now, together we
wash away bridge after bridge ancient
tide times tying us to
each other, copper in
the veins, copper in
the waters, copper in
scales on summer-run
steelhead returning from the present
sea, anadromous like you
returning too to me
from what was once sea
now high and dry
in the Telkwa Range.
Peaks are Sinemurian outcrops
rocks at work
again, somewhere close
to Dawn Redwood remnants
coppery red long ago mud sucked.

...

Deliver metallic prehistoric—tastes into me—we will head out

seaward together

see new red cedars

all new saline soils

JIM DODGE ✎

The Rub (A Charm Against Tough Winters)

I rub my wife's back
as she kneels,
arms around the toilet bowl,
puking her guts out
from the chemo for breast cancer.
I rub my son's back —
so tense it's trembling —
as he vomits into the kitchen sink,
hit so hard and fast by the flu bug
he couldn't make it to the bathroom.
I rub my dog's back
as he yacks up
the half-decayed squirrel remains
I warned him not to eat
but which looked so delectable to him
he snarled when I tried to take it.
I rub their backs
as they're wracked by nausea,
murmur, "Turn it loose,"
and "Let it go,"
inquire, "Has Ralph returned your call?"
and crack other bad hurl jokes
to lighten their spirits,
do what I can to help them through it,
and then clean up the mess.
I do it gladly
because they do the same for me.
(Except my dog, of course,
who humps my leg,
which I take as a kind of love,
or gratitude,
though it may be addled lust
or sheer canine confusion.)
Not that it matters,
because in the end
it all becomes
part of that tender, true, and deep regard
we feel for each other when we care
and don't mind cleaning up
the mess we sometimes make of it.

Learning to Talk

When Jason, at 3, said "beeber" for "beaver"
or "skirl" for "squirrel"
I secretly loved it.
They're better words:
The busy beeber beebing around;
the grey skirl's tail
swirling like smoke along a maple branch.
I never mentioned he was saying
them incorrectly,
though I continued to give them
the usual pronunciation.
One time he noticed, and explained,
"'Beeber' is how I say it."
"Cool with me," I told him,
"whatever you like."
But within a week he was
pronouncing both "properly."
I did my duty
and I'm sorry.
Farewell Beeber and Skirl.
So much beauty lost to understanding.

DANIELA ELZA ✒

the salt of being

is language an argument   against loss?
another tool   in the parlour   of the past?

where doubt   and fear   re-arrange
             the body's weight.

 curtains drawn as tight as a historic date.

                better to be stolen by
calligraphies of crow

*ente*rtain their flimsy nests   than feel
time's dull blade   against the throat. or

be caught in a winter's birch.   its limbs—
splayed syllables improvising sky. each day

rehearsing   the weather's fleeting moods
the wings   that briefly perch.

like   the frost's crisp message
the salt of being
        so briefly clings   to words.

yes   the words are   stubborn.   but are
willing   to wait for that freak   something
              that is   unnamed.

what adjusts the body's dial   as you halt
in the backyard
        before   your first bloom.

what spells   the sun's miniature thoughts
on the effervescent skin   of the fruit.

it is here
      that the soul is   calibrated.
the harvest—   secretly   consumed.

intimate harb*ours*

in the pinch   of humanity

                's loud vanity

the existential hole in the heart   grows daily.

trapped in an inch of exiled darkness

years pass   without awe

               without loves

                  without gods

life's hailstorms scatter   first d*reams*

truths get im*paled* on another

            's   astute par*lance*

drown in the thought of your own diminishing.

and you forget   the voice of   rustling rivers

the gentle blue features of

        what you loved

           what loved you back

without conditions.   between

the woman   dressed in meadow

        the man cloaked in sky

the genius of pure beauty   grips   the mind

at*tempts*   to bridge   the void with

a single act of   to *imagine*

          to *translate*

            to *touch*

in that small temple   between two

    before   the *demo*lition crew   arrives.

it takes an instant   to be seduced into

the invisible   the wholeness   of you

the idea of you   next   to you

  str*etched* across the sheets

                unfurled

     skin hums   with the still point

                 in which

the language

    of the immeasurable   pools.

This poem is a fake translation of sorts, inspired by a poem Alexander Sergeyevich Pushkin wrote for Anna Petrovna Kern. "drown in the thought of your own diminishing" comes from *thirsty* by Dionne Brand.

FABIENNE CALVERT FILTEAU ✏

For Wren, Turning Six Months Old

I.

A few hundred years ago your mother and I were lovers.

It was somewhere in the Middle East.

I asked for a dowry.

Her name meant soft slender flower. Imagine that.

Between my broad-bladed shoulders
I placed the flower—areola of turquoise flame, bleach-violet marrow of dusk.

This was her flesh
and wanting it
held fast for eternity
I pressed tight the flint bones of my heart.

Stone grated stone until her essence
squeezed out like blood.

On hard dirt, parched veins curled
into dust.

I snapped the headless stem in my teeth
and our children grew distant and dry.

II.

Does time in the body fold in on itself
like meandering fibres of muscle,
each story somehow woven
with the weft of every other?

And being spun
among other things
from stories in her blood,
what do you see

                                        between nose and skylight
                              when you look up from the change table
                                        to this woman, your mother?

III.

We came back siblings
in wet salt mosses of Scotland.

                                        I twinned myself to a brother.
                                        Her older eyes kept watch.

As she peered out at us
from behind eyes
and slippery skins of oaks,
we danced deeper into the woods, my brother and I,
crawled on our bellies into fox dens
and through slumping tunnels of mink.

                                        Her constant worry
                              irritated the hunting games
                                        of my childhood.

                                        She became
                                        just another
                              mother to run from.

Not until the old dock
sank to slime,
lake knitting a seam
above my nose,
and her minnowing fingers
fumbled for one last scrap
of me
to reel up
to the living,
did I come to see

she'd been born haunted—
the way some children are born
with cleft palates, twelve toes—
by the scent of sour wood, dreams
of gasping eyelets, alveoli drowned
by the muscled lung of the lake.

IV.

If indeed coiled
within the bodies of our mothers, time
is a ribboning cortex

then eras
accordion, collapse
in an amniotic room
no larger than a plump ripe pear.

Is it the passage—
hours crammed
against sticky walls
hot with blood
inching toward
cool steel light—
that creates beginning
and end, makes us pull
whorls of legend
into long straight histories
once we're born?

V.

The witch hunts. France, 1523.

Hill a sun-spangled
cottonfield of bonnets, a thousand smocked maidens
and heavy breasts of crones.

It all happened too quickly for us
to speak, hide tinctures, or eat words from medicine books
to feed our hungry unborns.

As the knife came down on the old country
necks of infants warped
on swelling cervixes.

Valley underbrush crackled with smoke, the uterine skin
charred to ash.

Behold burn scars of this exorcism:
heads of women tossed
like slaughtered hens among the pumpkins.

I turned to her
with pupils boiling.

Fire licked the heart
of her milk-calm resignation.

In an instant, the launch of an age
centuries long, crossing oceans,
where mothers laboured alone in hollow echoes
of cellars, their songs the shattered medicine bottles
of ghosts.

VI.

I look to you and see
a sky spun in raw cloud, oak meadows
of youth, forests of burning cohosh,
knowledge of the existence
of regret.

Your mother just popped into the minimart
for emergency diapers and snacks,

and ever on
those old valleys blaze,
parking lots reeking of diesel,
dogs licking oil swirls
from rain pools in the tar.

Slim

She wakes in washed-out light, her fly rod
caught in the door screen. Tree-bodied
woman, moose-toothed woman, her skin
has thinned to ash. She opens the woodstove to embers
gone blank, her feet brush the floor with their
numb toes lolling, she says, *This goddamn century
has turned me to paper.* Century
of euphemisms. Her fly rod casts a blazing opus
of curses at the sky. The last light scarlet.

EMILY KENDAL FREY ✒

When Do We Get to Ever

I can hear my body

making the noise

of memory. When we return

to the field,

I hope we find

the missing. I hope you

carry us

all the way.

And when our mothers

and our fathers

stay in their tall

branches, I hope we

shake instead.

All I want,

all I've ever wanted,

is that the red

bits break free.

MAXINE GADD ♣

Pemberton Rain May 20, 1968

        for the moon day
                day of the queen
                     you should have been there

    up at the rodeo
where they greet you, leaving
        under the apple and the willow
                to get out of the rain, a wreath
         of never-saddled horses
                 circling each other
                    in a victory dance
             that the sky had made the people leave
before the bronco busting

there was one little greek blue pony sold
        to a man with a lisp
And this other guy standing above and behind me yelling

               "i know that idjut of an injun
                  laughing at everybody"

the cabin on the shore

firelion
leaps
thru the window
butts
my elbow
makes
muddy pawprints
all over this page

light the lamp stoke the stove simmer the rice

looking for last night's salty singer
no nightingale
only
a gull
at dawn
tells me of the coast
a slope
that never eases

nicaragua
. el salvador

sailing to san salvador

do you believe
in the good wind
the water from heaven
sharks and turtles
struggling aboard
for your good soup

flying to san salvador

...
....
....
...

The Contralmirante Does Not Answer
My Amnesty International Letter

si.
well, senorita, i tell you
at least you send me
a polite and (fairly) clean letter
begging me for these lives.
i do take life seriously
as mine has been taken
bit by bit
daily
all these years

well, yes,
beating?
they used to make you drink yr own blood.
life was not easy, then, madam, even for a white.

my reasons?

go and ask General Ibanez de Tilleria.

ask him
about Margarita Sepulveda

what does it matter, madam,
who i
am?

what can it matter?

Berkeley, California

climbing dream mountain
steep and high
where intelligent lizards
greet yu
and that sensual
dog

and that handsome angel up again
        hovering on the blue
                just eight feet away

he has no apparent feet
and extends
a draped dish
towards yu

                        yu turn away
                    and look far down
                        and see
                    far far below

/sinister blue houses where from gullet-shaped windows piano music
        rises/played ever so lightly/by gigantic professors of napalm

even from here
yu fear
to catch their eye

            or to face the angel

KIM GOLDBERG ☙

Spawn

Under the bluest sky of the year, I stood at the edge of my world
and watched the flickerflashing churn of brimming life, the sea gone
white with sperm—the stench and smoky spew
of diesel-powered winches winding in their nets, beating
out the fish. I watched the shooting stars cascade into
the darkened hold to be later stripped of roe for
Japanese markets. The yawning emptiness between electrons
in the salty air—packed tight today with sirens' wail
and squaggling song from four thousand gulls and brant
aloft beyond the endless snowy drift of milt
whipped thick and scattered into bands of froth along a tide line
with no vanishing point at all.
All of this on the same day that the radioactive cloud
from Japan's nuclear disaster was scheduled to reach our shore—
all of us together in this self-made retroactive cloud
with no vanishing point at all.
We tipped and scattered clamshells in the froth, our lifeline
lost beyond the endless rift cleaving molten
rock and magma from four thousand songs and plants.
The salty air packed tight today with sirens' wail
in Japanese markets, while the yawning emptiness of our elections
echoes in a darkened hold to be later stripped and sold
as fish bait. We watched the shooting stars cascade into
a diesel-flowered meadow binding all our heads, beating
while it burned until the stench and smoky spew
was traded for the flickerflash of atomic churn. And the sea was gone
under the bluest sky of the year, as we stood at the edge of our world.

Urban Planning

Train tracks scrape past the sun-hammered miners'
shacks left over from the last
century. The front side is tarted up
as the Historic Old Quarter. But the backside
holds the story. Just ask the crumbling sunflower
sentries guarding the ass-end
of the Women's Centre. Or the weather-stripped
shiplap on the Bride's Closet next door
luffing like a beaten flag while some gunk
the colour of old blood drips
from a rusty pipe. I know this stuff
because I am now at a sufficiently advanced
stage in my daily rail-walking to support
a head-up gaze at my surroundings without
tumbling into the thorns. Beyond the
bridal store the shaling Occidental
Hotel and Bar prevails like an asylum
for the criminally insane. While across the
tracks a torn quilt pocked with bodily
stains lies splayed on a weedy patch
behind the Thrift Shop—a cardboard box
nightstand totters beside. She will
sleep here again tonight
unless chance finds her at the copshop on
the corner or perhaps in the bed
of someone she meets in the Oxy. And if he's
not too bad, maybe they'll get hitched
and pay a visit to the Bride's Closet (except
that's likely where her problems started—it's all so
cyclotronic). He'll probably keep
spending his nights at the Oxy, coming home
mean, talking fist-speak, till she ducks
out, goes to the Women's Centre, which
will be closed due to funding cuts, so she'll do
some dumpster diving in the donation box
outside the Thrift Shop till she finds another quilt
and a spot to lie.

Depot

Sooner or later
we all enter the slumber-soot
lair of empty lolling dragons, their grey tongues pulsing
under greyer sky. They wait for us behind the Beer & Wine store.
They are not anxious. They know time is on their side.

They wait for us
to reach this long unwind of shallow gut
slung beneath our storefront certainty, complete with ticket window
built this morning by stage hands.

They wait for our forward campaign,
our echo-location through crumbling
subterranean switchbacks, past leprous walls. The ceaseless
flaking off, the buckled carpet stains rising up to meet us, the hardened
rat feces, the crematorium of hot-boxed butts, the sickly flickerflash
of some stuck dream with a bad ballast.

(This is not The Hero's Journey,
it's just the way to the bathroom.)

Until we arrive
at the Stations of the Cross—all nine of them
(although the eighth is locked), each with its own shrine and scriptures
for our meditation, our reconstruction, our linkage to an essence
beyond our withered slumping selves. Give us Gandhi, Shakespeare,
Betty Sue, our Holy Trinity of chrome-and-tile-clad prophesy.

We open our hairy bodies
to offer our sacraments through the city's
creaking sewers, through abraded neural tubes, through
kerosene-soaked backdoors askew on sagging hinges. The turbulence
of our evacuation rips paper-thin nests made from mud and
wasp spit off their fragile moorings in our brains, leaving our two
hemispheres pasted together with nothing but a thick rebellious buzzing.

We offer the best
of ourselves, and the worst, the loosing of fury
held too long, of the startled calf culled from the herd, of yearning
that splits the heart like a bivalve to reveal its bluish pearl.

We empty ourselves
into the swollen catacombs aflood with
all the discarded turtles and goldfish and priests from centuries past.

We empty ourselves
within the steel walls rising two-thirds of the way
to the acoustic ceiling tile heavens.

We empty ourselves
into the tenements and crack alleys and cherry-red
Kitchenaid blenders, into uranium-tipped shells and kevlar vests,
into asemic chemtrails chalking curdled skies, into NCIS episodes
we have seen seven times, into networked cloud storage, mutant
crops, gorged soccer stadiums, tin buckets of radioactive mopwater.

We empty ourselves
into the vacant lot at the end of my street
where she returned to unity one summer night while the neighbours
heard wild animal screams and cranked up their TVs.

We purge it all
into the dark void cleaving specificity
from surprise, our greasy matted psyches chasing a prayerbook
butterfly that lets us think we can maybe grow light enough
to lift off and start over again.

Outside,
upon the planet's toughened surface, a young mother
(just a girl herself) with unknown backstory and knee-high boots
pushes a black stroller across the rain-sluiced platform
to reach the last bus.

JAMES GRABILL

The Idea of 2020

The laboratory door opens on Vajrayana emptiness. Any number of thoughts may be firing the same moment, some that may have been looking ahead to this day when they were just little risks to the future, long before the clear-cut Amazon under flat and deep overhead sun.

Exhalations of iridescent beetles and under-dirt badgers are mixed within breath, released as they were in trust of the place where we've found a heat-pulse chance, the queen of forests stretching luminous mushroom mycelia between roots of age-old sequoia and whale-eye winds.

This must be where the compass needle points to the sun, where taste of the air and water speaks to the living cells. For greater needs than birth have been saucering out of the gene pool, as this era of global hot spots launches out through time.

On the honey-hive prairie, innocence and inception continue. But the place no longer belongs to old assumptions of endlessness, and the present revolves on its sunken taproot of jaguars.

Iron Rails in the West

A little presence of the future has been going past in a locomotive puff of barroom smoke in which Bengali tigers are forgotten.

Sparks from the tracks fire off into branches, where iron wheels roll the traffic of sleep headed for the middle of this century.

Was that the smoke of a barroom, or a bedroom in which the groom and bride have been watching the casino wheel revolve around inequity and abandoned US trains?

It's a sure bet the Reno at the striking end of a matchstick will be flaring up eventually into immortality, the way molecules circulate around incomprehensible bonds broken for new bonds formed.

Collisions of coal locomotives massively erupt into boreal forests blazing and roaring against the back kitchen window, where a stranger is looking in through tiger eyes.

Once the high-speed train has pulled to a stop at the future metropolitan station, people will be climbing down from their coal cars, flooding the marble neoclassical lobby with their many voices from 2033 still echoing when they reach back into us to change us.

Emptiness Persists in the Forces of Matter

Fungi spread over the rock, drilling for millennia into it, turning out first soil which becomes a choosing ground for cells. Future prisming reaches back past knowing, to where neural acuity leans on nuclear core, as waking grows, aching for an end of suffering in the world.

Refrigerator-cool dogma falls apart in its caskets buried beneath mindfulness. Everywhere in molecular matter persists the unspoiled void. Vastness dogs the slightest shifts of sync, as it ever has.

Once coal cars have finally stopped passing over trellises of the spreading rake of the spectrum, will there be enough time? When darkened limousines are finished stalking the last money on Earth, how will the place look?

Mammoth industrial farms deplete the soil as we talk, however many minds may be firing at once. Still, hundreds of millions of heart-beat pulsations come thundering down around the sundance spine.

Lessons from *The I Ching:* **For the Mountain,** *Lheklhukxayten*
(The place to peel arbutus trees)

K'un/ The Receptive

"The attribute of the hexagram is devotion; its image is the earth."
[Even] "Its nuclear trigrams are earth and earth."

— —
— —
— —
— —
— —
— —

"The Receptive brings about sublime success,
Furthering through the perseverance of a mare."

"The mare is yielding, yet strong. So, likewise is the Receptive..."

The glade in the forest was filled with beautiful men
each of them astride a magnificent horse. These in turn
were arrayed with blankets of intricate design, their tails
and manes in multiple braids, colourful ribbons entwined.

They'd ridden since dawn, only arrived at midday
would relish but a few moments, respite in the cool
before joining the parade.

— —

"Just as there is only one heaven, so too there is only one earth."

They're standing on the mountain
up on the mountain, again today.
Standing up, up there on the mountain
for the children, the children's children,
standing for the generations,
generations yet to rise. Standing
up for all of us, up on the mountain.

They're standing
up there on the mountain.
They're standing
up for the mountain
for the forest
for the climate
for the planet.
They're standing up there
for all of us
up on the mountain
in the rain.

—— ——

"Nature creates all beings without erring...
It tolerates all creatures equally; this is its greatness."

Like reaching into your backpack, fingers
closing on a slug; the thrill of its slime insinuates
a chill against your hand.

Its gluey trail so resistant, withstands repeated
wipings, swipes across the grain of your jeans,
leaves its lingering glitter, tracing
the lines of your palm.

> Compare the ooze of bitumen
> *bit-chew-men, bitch-you-men*
> the thickened ooze of bitumen
> scraped across a beach, seeping
> from a pipeline, leaching into soil.

Instead, muse on the sweetness of persistent
forest slime, scent of rotting leaves, the slippery
trails of shiny slugs, black gooeyness sublime.

—— ——

"The good fortune of rest and perseverance depends
on our being in accord with the boundless nature of the earth."

This is the mountain where I knew the trails
spoke to ancient conifers, planted new trees
made outlandish love to you, my back against
the rough embrace of bark.

This is the mountain where we learned to walk
the shaded paths in silence, attuning ourselves
to the names of birds, knowing them not by sight
but by the joy of their songs.

The mountain where my children named the seasons
by their berries: salmonberries, huckleberries, blackberries, salal.
When to gather, which to eat, which to leave behind
nourishment of mercies for their brethren.

—— ——

"...linked with the tenth month (November–December),
when the dark power of nature brings an end to the year."
"... The Receptive is yielding."

Its broken lines are yielding,
can withstand the strongest wind.

The lines above portray old yin
those below, the young.

Together, they are stronger than either alone;
like a forest, they bend without toppling.

Against the storm they stand together,
protection for the earth.

—— ——

"Since there is something to be accomplished,
we need friends and helpers in the hour of toil and effort..."

They're standing
up on the mountain
on the mountain
in the rain.

—— ——

From a chapbook created to benefit the Burnaby Mountain Defense Fund.
Quoted passages are from *The I Ching* or *Book of Changes*.

SAM HAMILL

Habitations

for Ian Boyden

1.
Earth. Orange alpine lichen
slowly digesting stone.
Black earth.
Red earth, brown earth,
icy dust.

Canyons carved
through centuries
by water and ice.
Stone canyons,
mountains thrust up
by shifting continents.

Across the river,
the great trees
bend in the wind.
The living are the habitations
of the dead.
How small is a man.

2.
How small is the man
who reads the stones
and listens to the whispers
of the poplars?

How large is the heart
that measures the heart
of a man
with a handful of earth?

How much hope and sadness
is a man with a handful of earth
and a heart that unfolds
in the moonlight.

Listen closely
to the stars, to the flutter
of nighthawk wings,
to the silence.

In the moonlight,
the susurrus river
tells its secrets,
and the great trees shiver.

3.
The great trees shiver
and the river is laughter
and stones are polished
by rolling
when the river rises.

The patience of stone,
a congress of trees,
the witness of the moon—

If only human emotion
could be found
in the things of this world...

Even the river runs
out of time and drowns
in a desert or empties
into an ocean.

4.
An ocean
of time, vast seas of memory:
detritus
contains the seeds
of beauty.

He dragged from the river
an ancient cedar log,
half-petrified,
and used it to bind
a book. From shark-tooth, cuttlefish
and fossilized ear-bone of whale,
pigments for ink;

from stone, the soul
of stone, earth from earth,
transformed, transfixed—
from thistle and feather,
a made thing,
and yet it is an organism,
it has a life.

I say, the trees listen,
and even soil has mind.

5.
Soil has a mind
that legislates the trees,
each grape on the vine,
and the trees and wine define
the changing light
that burns inside the mind.

Roots of tribal memory
burn in solitude,
in the vast unknowing
of this known world.

Gneiss. Shale. Sheared marble. Schist.
Granite. Black coal
compressed into diamond clarity.

The whale's ear-bone,
the great tree blown down,
each turning to stone,
ground into powder for ink.

One hundred thousand years
in one small stone.
A feather is a magical thing.
And what does it mean?

6.
What does it mean
when one says, "The
stately poplar," or
"The noble pine"?

Scrub oak and loblolly,
cedar, aspen and elm—
each has its poet
with adjective and rhyme.

Because the river,
we like to believe, flows
through us, and
the more noble the tree,
the straighter our spines.

Down through hardpan,
two hundred feet,
through layers of basalt below the sea,
I drilled to tap a river in the earth,
a vein,
water for a home
of cedar and spruce.

Holy, the water; holy, the wood.

7.
Holy, these woods
reclaiming the earth,
rich in detritus
becoming soil.

Holy, the garden, its river
of stones, its moss,
lilies, and lace-leaf maples.

Should trees have standing?
Is the katsura aroused
by the arousal of its new leaves?
Its blood
surges.

Let the stones tell it.
Let the river sing it again.
Listen closely to the silence.
Listen to a language
not our own.

8.
Not our own, this earth.
For us, only the sacrament
of its fruitfulness,
and the great mystery,
and the mystery of our passing.

The tallest trees bend,
feathers in the wind,
and we marvel
at the sound of water in the moonlight.

Not ours, this mystery we enter,
this strange habitation.
The tide rises.
The river and the trees,
the stones and the man abide.

Tasting the wine, *terroir*,
is tasting the earth and sun.
Tasting the fish
is breathing the sea.

My brother, the blind poet,
uses his ears to see.
High overhead, the Southern Cross,
the River of Heaven, Ursa the Bear.

9.
We drift in the river of heaven
under the great bear
or beneath the cross
in a boat of dreams.

We drift in our boat of dreams
above the earth
and rarely touch it
unless it comes tumbling down.

And yet the trees
bear us up into the world,
the rains cleanse us,
and we eat from clay
all sacrament and abundance

before we return to clay,
to earth and stone,
gone like the cry of the thrush,
everything devoured and reborn.

10.
Devoured, devouring, and reborn,
the earth endures.

Here, where vast shadows
of bending trees
ripple on moonlit water,
there is a world at ease,

indifferent toward our boat of dreams,
our palette of temporal desires—

This time is measured only
by centuries of ice and fire
and by what the winds might bring.

Gazing up at these same stars
that inspired the artists of Lascaux:
the great void,
the mystery that is a hunger in the soul.

The bison gone, and the mastodon,
the butterfly that rode the wind
to Mexico and back,
the little bird that sang the dawn—
all devoured and reborn.

11.
Devoured and needing to be reborn,
the hungry seek a master.

Making the paper, grinding ink,
dipping the brush, the master says,
"Draw the sound of the breeze in the pines."
And, smiling, says, "Don't
be foolish enough to draw trees."

In the mind of a Buddha,
not even a flower.
Shiva the maker, Shiva the destroyer.

At the summit of a pass through the Alps,
high above timberline,
I knelt at the foot of a glacier
and peered down a thousand feet

at granite boulders in a creek,
and for a moment, knew
this ancient earth, orange alpine lichen
slowly devouring stone.

ENDI BOGUE HARTIGAN ❧

Dreamed Thoreau

I dreamed Thoreau drew frogs all night
on pale paper,
some numbered thousands
of frogs   Think it was a good dream
Say, I had bad or good dreams

Getting at something
what I wanted to say and what it seemed
seeming good.
I dreamed Henry David Thoreau drew
some number
down to the ones
I can't remember   Not the frogs themselves
but the fact of his   attention to them
however   blotched or poison blue
I had no faith

In our yard, an old sink with wet envelopes in it
The sky is a boy in
purplish rags singing

Thoreau is tied to the frogs, Thoreau is tied to the frogs,
and the frogs
are singing from the sink:
make it good, try hard

Arbitrarily

—I called myself myself though stemless. The river continued as a river,
   arbitrarily named Quench Root or Quartz Fork, an American name or
   claim, part personal, part vanished.

—I called the river something though. It was like taming a starling.

—Starling, starling, speckled night, yellow pecking mouth and knife, the
   name slipped into, over other names and we became, on the continent,
   continued.

—I called myself effaced, I called myself displacement then. I called myself
   a leaf or fin.

—No name so call it Quench Root, stained as if with chimney soot,
   swollen, swollen stem.

It was a church then

It was a church then it was a barn with church windows
then it was a photograph of a church-turned-barn.

It was a photograph of the church-turned barn
no longer standing and the standing
of the boy who just woke beside the photo.

It was a day then it was a church.
A boy wakes and feeds his golden fish.

It was a barn then it was a boy imagining barns.

I was standing in the barn which was a church
which was myself within a golden fish.

I woke then fed the boy.

It was a photograph of ghost towns then it was the ghost of the
fish in the sand of waking.

We played "ghost fish" by empty ponds.

It was a church then it was the ghost of the heat of the church.

A barn is warmer than I am.
The fish are the temperature of a church.

It was a boy with boy windows then it was a year with church-windows.

The whole building fell and had to swim its beams like ghosts.
It was a church then it was the fear of not having a church,
so it was the building of the church, the feeding of the fish.

No it was a barn.

It was a jellyfish

It was a jellyfish. It was a colony. It was that jellyfish proliferate in toxin-induced algae where larger life cannot—it was the proliferation of the word "soon" and rant at bus stops—jellyfish in milky seas—it was literal milk literal jellyfish happiness in these days proliferating, the imbalance of happiness proliferating, overflowing sidewalks—it was hands proliferating from the heart, tentacling and touching and dangling at a bus stop like a child—the proliferations of earbuds and volume, the small heart in the ear eliminating proliferating noise—his music makes him happy or imbalanced—it was the colony in jellyfish translucence in gum in glassy singulars in daily sums—a city expanding in multiples pop songs sounding like pop songs, car antennae that bend and shiver—it was the proliferation of nettles, interior cusps, the proliferation of time charts, exhaust fumes, forever strung in never strung in hope bloom coagulate and Gaga fuss—her loving makes her giddy and filled up—it was the ears proliferating from the brain and into it, the seams of the ears like the rims of a jellyfish or a cup—it was that people overflowed into signs and fins, signs of people overflowed into people, tentacle into sentinel signs of love surviving by proliferating out and out and out into the black sea, its equal pulses and rooms—

20 s. elegy

(after reports of a plane hitting a vacation house,
the family in the house having 20 seconds to react)

—20 seconds to retrieve what you can to collect 20 seconds
—go straight for the thing you intended to lift and lift
—we saw an eagle through a lens looking straight at our lens
—which was the best intention I lost it remembered the eagle
—at the end of 20 seconds the interval of eagles
—I said to 20 seconds I believe in the child and the eagle
—the mussel black darkness in which we slipped
—rehearsed or not we grab something before us
—the one with the impulse lived the one with the run-through impulse
—it started at 11 and ended at 3, the 20 seconds
—it started at the sun and ended at the sun
—go straight for the thing you intended to lift and lift
—lift the sea to the eyes of the child the eyes of the child to the sea
—which was the best intention I lost it remembered the eagle
—start at the 6 and end at the 10 but not numerals
—the mussel black darkness protected mussels thick
—it starts at the waking and ends at variations of waking
—go straight for the thing you intended to lift and lift
—the closest I got was lifting the child to the eagle
—lift the sea to the eyes of the child the eyes of the child to the sea
—at the end of 20 seconds the interval of eagles
—go straight for the thing you intended to lift and lift
—which was the best intention I lost it remembered the eagle
—the 20 seconds at the end of which inheritance blooms
—grab something to leave for the others grab eagles
—the one with the run-through impulse, light through a lens
—the eagle looked straight at the child and the child at the eagle
—time enough to forget who you are and run corners
—go straight for the thing you intended to lift and lift
—which was the best intention I lost it remembered the eagle
—it began at the 5 and ended at 9 and was over
—if you splice between the eagle and lens how many divisions?
—which was the best intention I lost it remembered the child
—skip what I said before about beginning and ending
—I refuse to think it ends where the 20th second ends
—belief is a kind of refusal then inspired by fissure
—skip the part about eagles and go to the child
—skip the part about death and go to the eagle

JARED HAYES ☙

blues mountain
rain drop
water sutra

for friends
andrew peterson
jimbo beckmann

*

you and
i are

dead already
already you

and i
are dead

all grass
the mountain

and rain
same grass

ravine and
runnel ravine

runnel rain
ravine runnel

rain heart
grass hears

sees open
sooth heart

sees song
sees rain

o mountain
skull heart

language traveling
on bones

blow blow
and marrow

smothering snows
all waters

the memory   .
off top

at foot
meandering channel

tide mountain
rush goddess

mountain ride
on on

cloud sky
o waters

mountains charge
beyond cantankerous

walking water
tho toes

love starve
splash bone

path practice
mountain walking

water walking
water mountain

water as
water as

water form
mountain water

moving still
water gait

we return
these leaves

water ordainments
when water

sees water
leap beyond

great mountains
sage edge

this one
this one

mountain this
one flowing
mountain

CRYSTAL HURDLE ✿

Ajar

IV)

We could start afresh. Leave the
missing fence boards rakish smiles lurid
ivy rings black aphids sticky honeydew
scuttling beetles upended plant pots
lichen encroaching neighbourhood
pocked porcelain crows feet enamel plastic wood
pubic tile ants march gorge poison
old paint shadows eczema hairline floor boards
kitchen clock 78 33 rpms cracked battery

Attempt time pitted color insecticide dehydrated sawdust
mildew voice floorboards stuttering angles
indentations wall-to-wall apparitions previous arrangements
foundation cracks the spirit unlevel
double bed leaks sheets mattress sag
quilts clammy shivering morning dark guilt

phone calls estimates questions value time
least three every complaint when
too late maintenance vigilant need
too big too much looming
repair buy anew?

House same age as marriage.

VII)

An open wall, the abandoned fourth wall
and what will we see staged?
Shakespearean malice?
Farce? Guilty couplings?
The angle of the door is small distraction.
We could see around and through it.
The air could be rich with our clapping.

VIII)

You make a better door than window
I have said in my sulks
but here it will not be true.
The door is a window
the open panes.
Please feel the silky panel
I have made for you, for us.
I have chosen the fabric, laundering it again and again.
Smell how sweetly.
I have cursed over the hem, slip-stitching
measuring and re-measuring.

Oh, you think this too obvious
a metaphor for our marriage?
Accounting for the coveted fullness
but lacking the formula
put in twice as much? three times as much?

I have bitten hard on the pins, drawn blood
and feasted on its metallic taste of penance.

Surely things have been gathered enough?
Your forehead is as ruched as the panel.
So the hem is a bit uneven.
Does it really matter?
Next step, panels for the windows too
I'll take down those wretched louvered blinds.
I will make the space ours. This could be a home.

GRAHAM ISAAC ☙

swiping the weather.

even as it stays hotter longer, more leaves skittering under bike tires in the
Central District, at a corner of a playground, hair salon and coffeehall. i
tap my device. rachel sits across from me with two fingers pushing up her
left cheek into her glasses, thumbing another device. the little green man
appears and disappears. the glowing red hand sometimes takes its place.
i was going to change the world again, but must bus to a jobhall where
people look up from their devices long enough to tell me if i should shake
or stir.

There's a limit.

                to how cretinous
There's a limit,
                to how functional
There's a limit,
                to dancing skills
There's a limit,
                to the efficacy of pirate costumes
There's a limit,
                to brave new acquaintances
There's a limit,
                to practicality of:

                              a feather duster,
                              a 401K,
                              Allen's patience,
                              your Hulu queue,
                              how long a glance is just-
                              how brief a glance can be, before:

                                                a slight,
                                                an aloofery,
                                                a pridewound,
                                                a papier-mâché
                                                cat.

How directionless would we be if we all knew how to dance,
but no one had that sticky blue tape to designate the floor?
There are leaves everywhere and people with scarves and that one guy
is too close to all the girls and that one girl has crazy eyes and slipping
clothes
and where, goddammit,

                          is the janitor?! *someone*
                                    has to set these things up,
jenga them to death.

CHELSEA JENNINGS ✒

Tonight the Trees

are braiding each other's branches. *Sister, sister.*
I sit at the sewing table, working
the treadle of a dead machine. What about

the cold suggests an absence, distance? In winter
the bedroom's too big, the heart's a root,
a beet, earth-in-the-earth. Outside the window,

apples fall hard and startle the lavender.
Under a finger—*phosphorous, lucifer, fire-inch-stick*—
summer's as small as the head of a match.

Swimming in the Dark

Night ripens in the bramble.
A true wheel turns the constellations.

Effortlessly we possess these bodies,
each in her windchamber. The sky

deepens in all directions, a darkness
embroidered by branches. Black

fabric, black thread. Black a season
unto itself, with room enough

for all our losses. Migratory shadows
in a downpour of stars.

Fall

Deciduous mood. Winter descends on the threads
of a screw. The wind is full of undifferentiated feeling,
the day's heat on its way out of the house.

Some spiritual presence, or some disturbance
of the ocular nerve, throws knives of light into one
corner of the room. Sun streams through the cinch

in an hourglass. Sun like salt, like sand. In this weather,
laundry surrenders. A window swings on its singing hinge,
someone sweeps the walk with a hard-bristled broom.

Before the Invention of Perspective in Painting

The sword and the sky are contiguous,
the halo of one saint the face of another.

Every leaf on the tree turns to be seen.
Angels never fall through the uneven

azurite, the hand stays grafted to the heart.
Devotion is possible. No thing behind

the color of a rock. Gold stops at the garment,
touches it, touches what skin is exposed.

Now mother and child need only one body.
The impossible bowl of wine will not spill.

DONNA KANE ❧

Resonant Frequency

The loon pipes air through its throat
and the mineral in me hums like the rim
of a wine glass, a microwave oven.
And like a party crasher on her third merlot
I want in on the conversation, my blood
burning up with bird call and breast bone.
I want to say, *this tremor reminds me
of what I am*. It's hardly true. My bones
could be scattered on the opposite shore
and still be vibrating to the sound of a loon.

Epiphenomenalism

which is the claim that awareness is
unnecessary to the brain, much
like a rocket booster's shadow
or Brad's shakes the time
Barry and I picked him up
from the plane. Twelve hours without
a drink, his hands so spastic he couldn't
light his Export A, fumbling
until the cigarette broke, the blunt snap
of its paper wrapper a piñata, bits
of tobacco on the collar of his coat.
At a bar with terry-clothed tables, Brad needed
both hands to lift the beer to his mouth—
the bottle wobbling like a spaceship
at lift off, the brain hunting correction.

They were no small thing, Brad's shakes,
the trouble they caused, the autonomy
of their dropped change, the unzipped fly,
the five beer it took for the brain to clear the tower
of its damaged nerves, and when it did,
it seemed not brain or thought
that leaned in to speak, but Brad who waited
for the mind to settle, for thought
to coalesce, Brad for whom awareness
seemed necessary, awareness
necessarily Brad.

Absorption III

It's not that the leg of a clothes moth couldn't break
but that the injury should be so confined,
calculated as a moon landing,
as though everything else had been ruled out—
no to the head, the compound eye,
no to the antennae, the thorax,
the abdomen, also no to the forewings,
hind-wings, right leg, middle leg, until yes
to the left leg singled and snapped, there
on the window ledge, the moth kneeling
as though bestowing an answer.

Which I take to be this:
to be chosen is no kind of truth.
And no comfort either.
If this is the heart of things, the smallest
of the small, wouldn't you
be disappointed? I poke the moth
and it flies at my touch above then
below the lamp shade.
Cruel, but see its desire to begin
again, see how the moth rises
against the singularity of its luck.

JOSEPH F. KEPPLER ✎

Poetics for People and Poets: A Seattle Location-Based Game Involving Art and Players. It goes like this...

First, two or three or more players agree to meet at a site like Michael Heizer's sculpture along the waterfront—*Adjacent, Against, Upon.* They then proceed to interpret the sculpture by imitating the three forms either through body positions or literary analogies or music or film or photography. They *record* their efforts on a portable device for viewing and comparing against others who have played SLBG or will play either SLBG or another location-based game.

Second, from this sculpture they move uphill to the nearby Seattle Art Museum's Olympic Sculpture Park (http://en.wikipedia.org/wiki/Olympic_Sculpture_Park). This is free-form for the players can select any sculpture to interact with in any way they choose. They can imitate, criticize, dance, etc., and then record their efforts on their device.

Third, from the sculpture park they move farther uptown to the Pike Place Market where they take in the rare small streets where automobiles take second place to pedestrians and where they can eat and talk their way through the Market or in a favorite restaurant there. Here they record their role as poets, critics, comedians, stars, etc. before they head off for their final destination.

Fourth, they walk to the Seattle Central Public Library where they will improvise their own tour as if they were librarian tour guides. Of course, they also photograph or record their efforts. (http://en.wikipedia.org/wiki/Seattle_Central_Library)

Finally they will upload their efforts to a social media site to compete with any other players who want to challenge the SLBG players with their artistic efforts at the same or different sites. The group with the most interesting art and poetry and criticism wins!

KOK KOX 🐦

ow

I saw
                                                     an
angel   burning   in the
        night,
                        hollow-eyed and   smoking
                                        ,

                                                                an angel
        illuminated,
                                eyes all

skull,

                                all

fire   in paradise   ,

        blind   and

                                                blinking
        in

                                                        holy

                                                        light
all night
                ,

angel

burned   in the   arms

of

skeletons

fucked in the ass by
           seraphim

     in
cemeteries
       endlessly
                                  with a sword,
   lost

       and
    ecstatic and insatiate

                     consciousness,
                 red eyed
                   and
naked

all night   waiting for a door
    to open to

                              Eternity
              ,

          burned alive   amid

                                                    shrieks of
                                                          the

forgotten   ghost   of   fire   ,

              hopeless
    soul illuminated   for a second

as heavy as the moon

—

sudden flash of

angel

naked and endless   ,
            angel
after death,

                  naked

                              soul

          whose love is endless   !

whose name is

                              Cocksucker in

                Heaven!

LARISSA LAI ✏

Excerpts from **"nascent fashion"**

*

case stated in white and white
nation born off a boat
all contention and emergent
clauses our ambulances
claim soggy sailors
slow separations

we dream tomorrow's murders
in dolby sound surround
advance guards tickets
stages side show
for sad dancers
simian simulations

we dot our lines
bloody signatures
traces name our children
tumble to other lineages
we forget our own

*

exposure unknown
agent arms open
and blazing
germ in the machine

o my lovely double
elsewhere and shining
fear the manoeuvre
my biochemical package
the secret mitosis of girls
nights thick with hot paste

ancient thrall of anthrax my old
acquaintance forgot at the mere touch

down and downier
hard copy broad and helmeted
sweet winged nike
dashes for the long needle

the anecdote
to save the grand narrative

*

it is dark and she
it is dark so thirsty and the smell
my body their bodies all this rot
this shit this vomit this blood

i didn't know i wanted
wanted the white bed
was that so bad?
white bed all crisp cotton and down
high posts a girl
i could yell at

i'd make her pay make her
anger i didn't see
the mirror myself ghost
white bed for ghost girl
wanted to help my parents
wanted a girl to rage at

this girl
is dark and she
so thirsty the smell
hunger long gone
air cries crises gap

in dark my body their bodies
old scarfaced bag who yells
at me i'll make her pay
the factory girl who pinches
the girl who cries who pricks her finger
who strains her eyes
the girl with chemical burns

the girl who suffocated
the girl with the severed hand

the girl i want
not this dark

the white bed in the glossy
advertisement i saw and the white
girl in the white dress so pure
i wanted
not this ghost

a girl to do
what i say

not me

*

this sorrow in the innocent
part the longing
imperialism's imperative scathes
we dirt even in revolution

desire awry
we force we blood we maim
she body she collective

in our innocent we search
culture's purgative rhetoric
as machines repetitive wilt spirit
as bones dig mass racial graves

our soft that works tears burns
dismembered and bleeding
she dark she poor
this litany all tongue-stuck and word-full
innocent digs for itself

absolute abstract
calls to body's miraculous
pulse and warm this soft

reproduces kisses even the hindered
belly blossoms

pretend a fresh garden
sing the charred cell's
delectable mutation phantom
pleasure of severed limb

chant the cancer regenerative
our brilliant pustules recall brine
of origin the new salt
futures a city of soft

biological meteors replicate
scale our feather our alien
innocent all damp and downy

*

my destiny's not a nation
i covet cloth
swathing of good citizens
drapery that tugged roads roman leading

america the dutiful
bolt fabric's long roll
to stitch liberty's desert camouflage

their cocky green misunderstanding
my fundamental duality
i love you i hate you
daisy chains my weedy uncertainty

poisoned well irritates
roots to sprout legs like
ginseng man the dark forest's

hot incubus shoots out of earth
to walk to truck to haunt
these night routes

in the hollow parts
of anything that moves

GP LAINSBURY ☙

from **Half-Life**

> *"...every man is capable of showing his contempt for the cruelty and stupidity of the universe by making his own life a poem of incoherence and absurdity."*
> —Gabriel Brunt

    ✻   ✻   ✻   ✻   ✻   ✻

I have nothing to say & I am saying it
in a kind of field poetry
From a position of openness to surrounding   context
Enveloped by a fine network of half-expressed thoughts & feelings
an atmosphere of such suavity difficult to resist   almost
w/out restraint

He arrives, unexpected, and possesses
a bare, wintry landscape, dotted w/ploughmen   plodding
        interminably
behind scrawny oxen

    ✻   ✻   ✻   ✻   ✻   ✻

The permanent condition of manufactured man
constituted of the sordid, its diabolical   subtlety
caught up forever in
burning & immortal
bizanteaten jaws of death
Scattered along stations at the
long end of the   spectrum
things are always going wrong   Naïve
voluntarism obscures operation of dark   forces

    ✻   ✻   ✻   ✻   ✻   ✻

Continuously firing gorgeousness
upon him she sprawled him down
w/out even a smile, hacked his heart

Later, weeping on top of the remains of her house
bemoans obstacles to intimacy

Helen: where necessity & beauty converge
in the playpen of erotic devotion
crisis heterotopias of deviation
begin to function at full capacity

   *   *   *   *   *   *

Writing in an obsolete medium
of witness & documentation
a "field of action" exhibiting aggression
to an audience   concealing amidst
its reflection of economic & class contradictions
deconstructive death rays
impelled by force grandiose, selfish & cold
throughout those dismal days
when the dead return to inhabit their former houses
needing to express their tendency to view   experience
through a lens of literary utility

   *   *   *   *   *   *

Walking through streets filled w/ghosts of early boy-selves
industrious, affable, having brain on fire

Everything leads to whatever follows
Bernouli's Encyclopedia of Imaginary Diseases
including a disdain for humanity as practiced
an Olympian desire for perfection over power
creating bridges between radical formalism
and a vaudevillian social platform

A strange state of mind, compounded   of shock,
unnatural calm, and grief sharpened   into anguish
by the complete wreck of earthly good

Party of animals/animals partying
amidst hyperbolic self-imagining
repudiates all notions of authorization
emptiness w/a few things arising   in it

Glorification of energetic stupidity
a methodical tool designed to subvert

expectations of bourgeois readers
suspended in a doubt-like world

There is no escape from heaven
that large brothel called Aquitane,
its hatred of everything that doesn't
relate to literature the proper setting
for epic scale brain warfare among   poets
codependent & entangled sadomasochistic
perpetual institutionality of avant-garde practice
the mania for phrases drying up the heart

*   *   *   *   *   *

"If anyone is sleepy let him go to sleep." –John Cage

Write as short as you can, in order
of what matters, as if your parents are dead

Your loneliness is a complex group dynamic
to keep the mind alert but empty

Practice: a syncretic poetics of ingenuity & invention, collage & palimpsest
where music invades the sentence
at the vulvic gateway to *Archaos* dreams leak
and the dead return, but only if you love
grim deeds & moral panic, that aridity
required for the production of genius
self-involved and unable to draw joy from the world
its pitch, timbre, loudness, duration
glorious penetralium locating us as part of an intensity
not an instant lost/
                     doing what must be done

Women edge away from smell of hopelessness
the fraudulent imposition of *Eros* over *Ananke*
minor, deceptive & extended *detournements/*
         normal marital hatred

Devote one's life to beating one's head against that wall
collecting, hoarding and archiving laws & people
ambitionless setting oneself up on verge of ruin
a maggot on the corpse of its revisionist masters

Narcissistic aversion to seeing oneself as permanently ill
divination algebra connects holographic sense to
useless primordial reality of soul

Prepare for the next dumb blow
barest inkling of joyful wisdom always
overwhelmed by cheap/
                  teenage nihilism

     *   *   *   *   *   *

"If the mind is disciplined, the heart turns quickly from fear towards love." –Meister Eckhart

Sincerealism of the workless world of work
seen through rectal eye of disorientation
everything happening at once, heavy
eyes & rain, thick head & ground-fog never
thinking get some of that love

Transcend! sensitivity to rejection
leap over the wall of self after logos
abstract rejection of epic encyclopaedism
isomorphic speech-times closely correlated
with higher whole-system productivity
its typically ironic and tightly disciplined nature
is breathtakingly beautiful

"Just because it's New Year's Eve doesn't make this in any way excusable."

Guilt-ridden literary forensics your
disturbing & conscious complicity
in his long-anticipated breakdown
talking too much bullshit, tapping feet,
facial twitches, not looking directly
into eyes when talking   shades of Duncan '63
              Olson's blazing sun
fragmentary images a terminal moraine
left behind by passage through conscious-   ness

Everything had been tried
and he just couldn't stand it

                        any more

ROBERT LASHLEY ✏

Thirteen Ways of Looking at a Motherfucker at the Club

(after Wallace Stevens—Mwahahahaha!)

I.
Among twenty bros at the club
the only thing moving toward my cousin
was the eye of the motherfucker.

II.
I was of three minds
like the IQ
of the motherfucker at the club.

III.
The motherfucker at the club
whirled in the autumn wind.
It was a small part of some corny bro dance.

IV.
A Maxim magazine and Axe body spray
are one.
A Maxim magazine, Axe body spray
and a motherfucker at the club
are one.

V.
I do not know which to prefer,
the time when the motherfucker at the club
says to my cousin
"Girl, I want to sop you up like a biscuit."
or
"Girl, you look good enough to season greens with."
or
"Girl, if your left leg is Christmas, and your right leg
is New Years, can I visit you
between the holidays?"

VI.
Bros filled the window with
barbaric glasses of liquor
a rapper drank on BET.
The motherfucker at the club
drank them, to and fro
an indecipherable case.

VII.
Oh thin bros of Seattle,
why do you imagine that you
could put Rohypnol in my cousin's drink?
Do you not know my juvenile assault record
when you walk the feet
of the young lady around me?

VIII.
I know Noble accents
and lucid, inescapable rhythms,
but I know too
that if the motherfucker at the club
gives her that drink, I will catch a case.

IX.
When the motherfucker at the club
flew out the window,
it marked the many circles of black around his eye.

X.
At the sight of the motherfucker at the club
flying outside the window,
a bawl of euphony cried out
What did I tell you? What the fuck did I tell you?
If you put your hands on my cousin again
I will cut the bacon off your back and fry it
to your goddamn daddy.
I swear before god, boy,
I'll bust your head to the white meat
and kick you up and down this block
till your ass tore out the frame.
And what the rest of your bros looking at?

Which one of your motherfucker's wanna axe
the dentist to get they teeth fixed.
Don't let the smooth tweed fool you!

XI.
The motherfucker at the club ran past downtown
with a busted hand.
Once, a fear pierced him
in that he mistook
someone else
for a person who was driven away.

XII.
The wind is howling.
The motherfucker at the club is somewhere in a corner.

XIII.
Grrrrrrrr.

The Little White Dude with the DJ Quik Jheri Curl

(After William Carlos Williams' "The Red Wheelbarrow")

So much depends
upon

a little white dude
with a Dj Quik jheri curl

riding his ten speed
down the block

trying to get his baby momma
at the hair salon

a sandwich.

CHRISTINE LECLERC ☙

from **Oilywood**

for the collaborators

1

We listen to water.
We go float in it.

The ocean makes us giggle.
  We giggle when we're in it.

But no matter how advocacy voice
demands our sketches, the future is far
from shapeless. The future is already
flush with months, minutes and—

hear something

—

assholes. It has power, movements
and press releases. And it's full of
soundtracks to make you feel you've
just seen a movie, like your life is
something—

hard to leave

—like a supertanker.

Interim service begins on Midcontinent Express pipeline.

Kinder Morgan announces open season for crude oil shipments
        on Cochin pipeline.
Louisiana pipeline in service.

Rockies Express pipeline begins service on Rex-East.
Kinder Morgan completes first commercial shipment of biodiesel in US—

linger

                   —on
                   Plan-
                   tation
                   pipe
                   -line.

2

There are many ways to feel
and the way to feel doesn't matter exactly.

Kinder Morgan announces closing of—

                   make out

El Paso acquires more interest in Colorado—

fish on rocks

        —Interstate Gas Company.

Kinder Morgan and Energy Transfer place all of Midcontinent
      Express pipeline into service.
Kinder Morgan to acquire gas treating—

throw sticks

—assets from Crosstex.

Kinder Morgan begins biodiesel shipments—

for our doggies

--on Oregon pipeline.

3

About a mine site—pit nothing-
power. Watching tractors build
moats to keep us from running for
miles through bitumen and tailings
lakes, crossing high voltage lines,
obvious as—

fog-drizzle

—to keep us from
stopping anything more, which was
little, but televised, so something of
trouble.

It's not a thing to write about from
the ground. From a helicopter, maybe.
Or a big city building with satellites on
the—

rock skip

—roof. Especially if you're paid
to do it, you can begin to say things
that make the story about something

other than people in yet another
mode of gasping.

Kinder Morgan completes natural gas acquisition, receives
PHMSA authorization to operate new pipelines,
honoured by EPA for participating in natural gas STAR
program.

Last leg of Rockies Express Pipeline completed: all 1,679 miles
in service.
Kinder Morgan and Copano Energy Announce New Eagle Ford
Shale Pipeline Project.
El Paso to present—

star-shot

—at RBC
Capital Markets MLP Conference.
Kinder Morgan promotes natural gas executives.

Kinder Morgan Announces Closing of Underwriters' Over-
allotment Option.
El Paso Expects Continued Growth.

It wasn't easy to go to all these beaches. Some of them were hard to get to. And some of them were full of foreboding, like the beach in Burnaby with orange sand and jogging executives. It was one of the last trips I made. I wanted to see the Kinder Morgan terminal with my own—

flickering sunset

—eyes.

The path tapers off into something just beaten through a twisted patch of woods, and if it hadn't been for the fact that a woman who looked like she could karate chop a shipping dock was ahead of me on the path, I might not have pushed on.

There were leering men at the edge of the wood. And the woman. And her dog. And a mostly disappeared strip of shore. And the rising tide, and the rocks, and my crap shoes.

In the end, from the rocks what you see is a pipe.

But I wanted a picture. So I took one with my phone and moved closer. And no one stopped me and no one cared.

I went closer, and the pipeline was white. It jutted out beyond the edge of the dock and it didn't make a sound. I wanted to take another shot as my shorts wicked wave water.

The leerers and the karate chopper
and her dog were gone.

And my phone was gone.

It was stupid to have dropped it. It fell
out of my pocket.

But the water crashed harder. My feet
went cloven and my eyes went like a
dog's nose. I held branches and flew—

nooned

—across the
rocks. There was an orange light in
the shallows, by the woods, as the
waves tossed my phone in the sand,
my phone still taking pictures.

Kinder Morgan Copano joint venture will provide more
gathering, processing and fractionation capacity to Eagle
Ford Shale producers.
El Paso provides annual outlook, expects growth.

Kinder Morgan and Copano enter Eagle Ford Shale Gas services
agreement with Anadarko.
Kinder Morgan enters agreement with Massey Energy,
announces oil storage acquisition and—

went there

—joint venture.

El Paso agrees to acquire more interest in Southern Natural
Gas Company, announces exercise of underwriters'
option to buy more common units and acquire more
interest in Southern Natural Gas Company.

JARED LEISING ✏

There Is One

word you can't shout
in a crowded theater.
Just seven you cannot

say over public airwaves.
I count fifty you can write
upside down on a calculator.

And over five hundred
you best not Tweet or post
without Big Brother

raising an electronic
eyebrow. Like "pork,
cloud, subway, delay."

This list makes me hungry,
makes me stop off at
the Cuban sandwich shop

on my way home. I order
Caribbean Roast coated
in a generous marinade

that would make
even the Department
of Homeland Security

reconsider "embargo."

Keep Portland Weird

Keep your Voodoo Doughnuts,
    your Velveteria
Keep your Church of Elvis
    open for ever.

Keep your city block's worth
    of books in print
and I'll keep this short. Like you,
    I'll opt out

of terrorism task forces,
    I'll build ten bridges
across a river. Just promise me
    you'll keep your

Acupuncture Project up
    and running, alongside
the Urban Iditarod and your
    City Commission.

Keep the change and I'll start
    bombing churches
with yarn and hills with bikes.
    Keep your sales

taxless, your water fluoride-free
    and you can keep
pumping my gas; just keep
    your distance

from Seattle
    an easy drive.

CHRISTINE LOWTHER ☙

Raven

Raven cannot be co-opted
by a seedy drinking joint
down at the docks.
Not by a fanged nightclub
in a TV vampire series,
nor by Stark Raven, a prisoners'
rights show on alternative radio.
Not by a person's name, given or chosen,
nor by Raven: western Canada's one-stop
source for truck accessories
since 1977. Wide load.

Air sieves through black feathers,
stroking the clouds, the sound
of fast flight.
Fighting mid-sky, claws up
to repel persistent crows,
spinning over, claws down
to plague eagles:
their young scream like vixens,
their elders call like evolution
cupped in hands of air
echoing off mountainsides.

In some places ravens are so plentiful
their voices thicken and fall,
new calls come from
the ground — stand still and feel them
speaking in your soles,
vocal vibration, your bones their microphone.

When the open palm of sky
holds out a sound not recognized,
it will be Raven's call, melodious,
a voice like caves,
darktime in daylight,
reminding.

A cry that can sculpt skies,
cut through winds, carve
a whole language
from one bird's shaggy throat.

Pondering British Petroleum in Florida

Oil has been drilled. It spills all:
The numbers soar,
unlike the birds anymore.
Three hundred sea turtles,
shells slick under my caress. Hatching season.
Inside thousands of hatchling-turtles,
their organs marinate in me.
According to the anchorman, only
one "blackened" dolphin.

> Water columns stifled with the blob,
> dog walkers' shoreline a killing field.
> Dreams of ruined bodies covering
> planes, cars and boats, coast to coast.
> Cormorants and herons draped oozing
> over my prized Suzuki fourstroke outboard.

Facebook friends post images for the nightmare files
—some nameless seabird on its back
swirling in tar, black feet in the air
because the anchorman only said nothing,
for three weeks, while we waited.
Volunteers were turned away
unless willing to sign
contracts with the oil company.

Time to get off-grid, go home:
lower the motor, check its oil
carefully (without dripping),
start ignition. Replace guilt
with responsibility. Commit
to healing old injuries
enough to take up paddling again.

> Think about attaching a sail.
> Imagine joining covert clean-up crews,
> the swing of the shovel,

triumph and despair
with every capture-rescue,
a kind of pleading
with every pull on the rake.

I hold you in the palm of my black hand.
A planet's blood belongs buried,
embedded in rock,
soothing friction between fossils.
You think I wanted release
into this fluidic expanse of salt?
Yet I like being here,
the heaviness almost gone;
I move and there is light above me.

Out my window the resident merganser
and her seven ducklings pass,
a clean line of serenity. Begin
typing

Ahab Mayhem

With whale fat spilling all over the deck
what makes him so
American mad
so cerulean cruel so human
so like the jaws of wolves on fat
lust for the hunt on a quest like hate
(also like ambition) so American Emperor
nailing a gold doubloon on deck
so man of his own ship hanging the heads of two whales
dripping sperm (the smell of whale fat)
identifiable to even the so like a virgin green beginner:
Ish—you make the rope seamen use for hoisting
and meet the queerest creatures of the sea
and him, he gets so vapid vision quest gain after gain
so supine brain dead so interior mad so exterior far away look in his eyes
then to the lookout says he, "ay!—see him yet?" Ahh, ivory leg Ahab
digging in the deck a divot of his very own, a mark that fits
his alabaster leg fashioned from bone of whale, feeling bucolic
You Ahab! You ruin us all with your American ambition, roaring Ahab
boiling point Ahab, balls to the wall Ahab
the importance of sperm inconsequential as if
the magic white flukes of any white whale would do as well
but for this nacreous as the new moon hue
used for lighting lamps and making hair brushes
we endlessly sail the sea sipping Nantucket water
watching for the great white spewing that by now we all want to see
his hump like a snow hill then cut the anchor and chase and chase
and chase all over the surface of the ocean until we meet
the eye of the whale and see him:
Ahab in a whirlpool flushed like a man
into the depths of damnation black vomit
like an enemy of the sea born creatures who never thinks
but only feels home far from Nantucket and minus half a leg
he chases and chases and chases until an element emerging from the sea
sucks us under and the entire Pequod yawning for help while the ocean
    was gulfing
while watchful birds were winging the sea air and splintering shrieks
    escaped their beaks

the sea moves over lost ship shards and bones which were once like us
five thousand years ago and I know
I want to live as the ocean floats me about in the cool deep
and while the surface of the sea was recomposing itself
the peace and quietude of thinking and remembering
Ahab previously fishing men out of creamy pools and shark jaws, careful
    of his own three limbs
his alabaster one too
his mad tethered heart and hands and all the stars leading up to it
he came to us like that
mad without sleep, mad with resent and with the wind in revenge
that hard irascible puffing at his sails
that secret interior madness and how it became a furious exterior
"Oh, lonely life on lonely death!" my American mood for hate's sake
clinging to wood like a man who wants to live to tell
I am
clinging to the coffin of my mate
All dead I think
I am
to become a fire in the heads of hello my name is
Ishmael

The Very Insistence of Hello

for Gregory Laynor

*A bird's singing is perhaps the nearest thing to repetition
but if you listen they too vary their insistence.*
– Gertrude Stein

the very assurance of one's hello
the very essence of one's hello
the very nature and or incandescence of one's hello
the very hello of one's hello
and the very commerce of one's hello
as one's hello emerges from the bellows
below one's hello and then there's
hello again and hello good-bye
the songs of hellos one blows in the wind and sand
hello!-hello!-hello! becomes the verb hello in trees
and the songs of hello becoming o-shell-o, o-shell-o
and the if hello or the haunting hello and the hollering hello
and if you want we can even do some of these hello's over again
like bellowing hello and helloing hello and propelling hello
and the emerging of hello from the belly hello again hello
have we gone into the beyond hello yet again hello haunting hello
again in the trees like wind and hello the moon and hello they call me
howling hellooooo—oo-oo—ooooo——he—e-lloooooo—oo-
    oo—oooooo

Spider Noises

as early as 4 a.m. I can only suspect the mutable noises of spiders
their continuous threading, slipping and jumping
"to make a net a lot like a baseball glove" I tell myself the changeable morning
    the sun
coming up only to stay, I silently say, "behind the clouds" "a bright gray"
the spider crisscrossing the window pane knows better and launches his body
    again and again
I wonder—waking to the morning white—what are spiders made of?
suspicious of the sky I tell myself "leaning, reclining, bending, yes bending"
today I will only think about birds eating spiders eating birds eating spiders
and the cats that watch them, carnivorous creatures, creatures in trees
and creatures with silky threads I think and look out
to the Olympics, the Cascades, and Rainier and see
all around the glooming blue, thick like paint darkening
all around the day the leaning clouds gathering
to say to the mountains "today we will change you forever"
listen I'm not crazy, but this emerged from the belly of the mountains
"I am a Walrus!"
"I am a Walrus!"
"I am the Eggman"
"Coo Coo Ke Choo! Coo Coo Ke Choo!"
and the vibrations of the mountains were felt
twanging those silky threads on all the window panes
and all the branches between bushes and trees and crevices of cars and trucks
and trash and I hear the quite early morning murmur of Seattle speaking soft
indistinct stories of the very oldest particles as they stand out there in time
a broken hymn becoming something else, an implosion within a non-air
    system of angelic orders
their bluish muffle a breathing of technology,
the way the throat short circuited absolute beauty over us,
angry hoary breath it has, every season it becomes unbearable
too frigid to tell love eating love is a symptom and that no one wanted to know
birds, bats, foxes and butterflies are all involved in this February, March and April

DAPHNE MARLATT ✆

"a mesh of force"

moth (er) wings twilit you mothing a study of *motte* older than butterfly great
grey scales you drew sharp-pointed jags clothing her slenderest arms

15 for moth, 84 various mothers, goddess to motherwort

featherlike delicacy

seated on scroll bench mirroring rail (tracks far off) i-beam only I dis-
connect in so solitary back to the world's eyes gauging that naked
nape tender as geisha kimono slips shoulders delicate spine

A rustle of hurt
A whisper of wings

La Parque manqueé

you spiny urchin say,
near smashed her interior
coming out

she, slow-cooled exterior
perfect the *cool blaze of her*

stress concentrated within

closed in her own bologna bottle
Sibyl wings folded in
what you cannot
forgive

disuse

––––––––––––––

O O O
felia

who took your portrait?

all misty greys, except that black clutch of dried leaf/berries attached
(attacked?) to white mantilla wrapped   cold lace   *perfect mouth*
pearl skin madonna-lidded eyes and luminous   unblinking   gaze

O mirror photo

ritratto in retreat
behind that face

giving nothing
away

_____

an immaculateness
that saturated

all her belongings, an
aura of snow

— in context please, this follows my note about her being a seeress.

— you don't say much about *these mysterious gifts* except to say the first
   of these is beauty. how did that mark her a seeress?

— to live with someone who safeguards her beauty…well, she couldn't.
   beauty involves being seen. after he died there was no one for her, no
   one who could see her the way he had.

— so twenty-five years of seclusion then? even for you?

— *immaculata.* for her there were no greys, only black and white.

_____

self-imposed purdah
self enclosed in
myth she was living
amid the alien corn
declined at table

    grass benches of Vernon's
    lake terrain home/
    sick for Rome

just Pleasant Valley Road

    grief squalls driving
    within four walls

raison d'être for here
politic, principled
vision gone with him
scholar of Islam turned
valley orchardist

    in light of economic
    collapse, war

"The Lord is near to
the broken-hearted..."

crevecoeur not simply
folded wings
glass sharded now

refus!

this wasn't what she chose
or you, this Okanagan
zenana alone

_____

— you see from the outside only, one face of it.

— "self-imposed purdah" woke me up the night of the lunar eclipse.

— there are various darknesses. she was my dark guide through grief.

— but your phrase for her, *a mesh of force.* why "force"?

— perhaps *the force that through the green fuse drives the flower*—that poet knew love's destructiveness.

— and you did flower, after she died.

— ah, the warmth and light of friendship, of talent set free…

— later, looking back you said those twenty-five years enclosed with her were hell.

— yes, hell on earth. but i had that earth, that grounding in my father's books. he taught me to think. she did too, on her Catholic terms. the force of her devotion, of seeing through the apparent, past one face of the moon—she taught me too.

— so that was your stem?

— or if you like, the long neck of the bottle i cracked. she couldn't.

———————————

J.W. MARSHALL ✒

A Skagit

The sun is down about all day.

The field's in its gown
of snow geese.
Each the mounds the gullies.

It rains such that
        the sky
is all a wrist and
knocking—

Wake up,
little energies, come out.

Is crowned, the field, in geese-shaped lanterns.

Is soggy, the field, and just for you
who get this time to be
tulips.
        Who get this time to be a daffodil.

Not Let Across the Hood Canal

Like public funded art
it is a threat

Makes traffic stop
because
the tender's opened up the bridge

The surfaced submarine is heading out
that tendon in
the global lurk and shove

At the railing oohs and ahs

The hills around
are green as stacked green towels

Children roar to life
like tassels yes the wind
will make you okay teary

A Trident sub
is canary black is
black is solitary as a mile marker

We have everywhere to be
and have to wait

Strolls

Out walking somewhere
I bowed my head for branches
and to dogs and cats

        &

I went without a hat
which wasn't a mistake
        The rain
was wrong and later it
apologized

50th & Sunnyside

On the corner there's a button that when pushed
        eventually sends
traffic a red light. Should you want to cross.
                Just because
no cars are coming you don't have to
cross a street. Even when
        you're wet and grim and cold you don't
have to.
      And if
you've pushed the button and drivers have
stopped their cars
                you don't have to walk.
                  Standing there is how
the pedestrian runs a light.
Show your hands palms up like
          you're offering a length of rope
        which is the universal symbol for
excuse my failure to act correctly.
Your face should indicate you'd lost control.

JERRY MARTIEN ☙

Now the Ice
   – Glacier National Park

Thousands drive here / participate in their / vanishing.

We fly / rent a car / take each other's pictures with / photogenic pale greeny-blue lake / white water cascading down rock. On the mountain flank / small figures along the trail / pilgrims to a disappearance.

The Americans they will say / worshipped Nature / worshipped Money. A restless practical nation so engaged in / present business / they lived by burning their past / their future.

At the park interpretive center the young ranger / assures us it's not really / glaciers / their effects are all / visitors want to see.

Above the lake / remnant of a million winters. Ice / on rock / carved by ice / with rock.

1908 George Bird Grinnell / says to the President / protect these 150 magnificent glacial peaks from mining / development. Crown of the Continent / says Grinnell. Bully / says TR.

Says Great Northern brochure / America's Alps. Visitors arrive by coal-burning locomotive / motorists tour in gasoline-powered automobile. Stay at Prince of Wales Hotel / built by a business buddy of William H. Taft.

He got 160 acres / Blackfeet land @ $25 / acre. We get tourism / reservation living / 27 diminished masses of ice.

First week of August / up to our freezing knees / binoculars scanning the distant shore. White ribbons of water / fall from the crags / splash against rock / into thimbleberry / huckleberry. On the high slopes / mountain sheep / more pilgrims / soon grizzlies / coming down for berries.

To the ranger I say / I'll tell my granddaughters / come visit soon. Later / might be too late. Yeah / he laughs. See 'em while they're / hot.

   water never so blue
       as the blues of their melting

Composition as the Way West

Not the news of the day but its composition. Not its politics and organizing but its being organized. The way nature composes itself. Things finding their place. Right hère. Put your little foot. Hoof it. Shuffle off to where the buffalo are gone. The days dedicated to following the ghost herds. The heard thunder of their hooves. Having it their way. Wandering the plains. The plain truth. The opening. The horizon. The herds seen from the wagon train westering. Following the way. Way to where west commences. Riding the absence of fences. Sentences connecting the way east and west connect. Nowhere you can go that is not the trail. The path. Pathological progression of wild horses. Riding ridges scouting for wild message. Down there the wagons on their linear course. Getting somewhere. Oregon or bust. Settle down. Raise buffalo. They raise hell with fences. The farm fails. Form fails. Nothing ends or begins we just run out of continent or time or breath and call it home.

to a northern spotted owl

from the meadow
a dark shape
soundless
rises into the douglas fir
beside my tent

branch bending
with her weight

last night around the fire
naturalists and nature-writers
doing owl calls

I try the basic
five-hoot greeting

she turns her head
a fraction of how far it
could turn
regards me
opens her
wings and
glides one tree
over to an
empty campsite

white-dappled
woods-dark
feathers upturned
at the tips for
silence

her temperature
the owl-man said
depends on
where she is
in the canopy

she wears the forest
warm and dry
in the tree-top
cool and wet

down here
where she hunts

she swoops
onto the meadow
strikes
rises with
empty talons
returns to the
forest edge

besides mice and
voles and canopy
she requires a
new cavity
in an old tree
every year
baby owls
like humans
leave a big mess

what she gets
is industry talking
higher rates of rotation
lower percents
of retention
with buffer zones
and off-season
campgrounds

exile in our
own land

when winter
comes colder
& summers
broiling hot

we'll all wish
we had a
forest to wear

Breitenbush, Oregon

SUSAN MCCASLIN ☙

The Power of Vegetables

"With an apple
I will
astonish
Paris"
said Paul Cézanne

though it wasn't just the apple
but the multiple seeings
one perspective from the right
another from the left

another from above
another from below
and so on
all in one apple

a cross-dimensionality of appleness
in an ordinary apple
one might use for pies
or apple sauce

"The day is
coming
when a single
carrot

freshly observed
will set off
a revolution"
he quipped

I'm still revolving in my dreams
        the matter of the carrot

Seeing Seeing

Whether an apple
                     new or just turning to decay
       (waxy oblong rotund)
           or the fallen-into-stone bodies of enormous bathers
he painted interbeing:

the wild and fluid mergings
              of world with eye

(his wife Hortense
          the gardener Vallier)

not just his reflections on subjects
            but his engagements
              with the temperaments of things leaving

staying with transience to the end
          (which might be why so much in his work is
          unfinished

                  for what's an end?

Seeing into essence   gave him patience
            or patience gave him the power

(His paintbrush was his meditation mat)

His productions
       seemed to the Salon de Paris
          travesties of crudeness
not produced
          (but emerging)

He didn't mind showing his brushstrokes
                globbing on the paint
didn't care about sustaining
         any illusion

that he was engaged in anything other than
        one trowel after another

                at being

He is flint
    when it comes to staying with the process

which is why I love him
    (perhaps just what one shouldn't say in a poem)

his determination
      not to care about getting his work finalized   approved

his letting go   into
           sheer presence
                shearing away at time

    seeing into the process of seeing

      (If he had been born blind he would have seen)

Epistolary Poetics

You have chosen the brush and you have done right, because everyone must follow his bent...But allow me to mourn the writer who dies in you...Instead of the great poet who is walking out on me give me at least a great painter... (Émile Zola to Paul Cézanne, Paris, Aug. 12, 1860)

In his early letters to Zola it's clear
                Cézanne could write
lubricating his word-horde
                   with Latinisms, Horatian epigrams, translations
challenging Zola to produce *bouts-rimés*

Okay, says C, send me some alexandrines rhyming
Zola et Voilà
metaphore et phosphore

Hanging over the exchange
I want into their game

When C signs off as
        Paulus Cezanius
to his carissime Zola
           just sign me up for
           some Bohemian doggerel
           & orthographic phantasmagorias

Now it seems the art of letter-writing
has almost died
though occasionally
our emails shine

If not for Cézanne's
insistent eye
he might have
answered his poetry Muse

Today I celebrate
Cézanne the painter
and the painter who died
in me at twelve to birth another
poetry slave

FRANCES MCCUE ✺

Steeple River Faith

No need for a church
In a town with a river

Boys turn out fishing
And leave the ball fields

Empty: bleachers vacant
As pews on sunny afternoons

Reels of the faithful
Danced at the tavern

Honkey-tonk sermons
Told them how to live

In songs that twanged
Their innards while steeples

Hovered over Sundays and
No one minded the call.

In a town like this
Anything could be fixed

Right down to the stone
the river of the matter.

The Trio

If you don't want to live in a black and white world,
Don't take a cop to the dance.

That's what my dead husband told me
When I put a cup to the wall and listened.

What about this new guy, is he a liar?
And my husband said from the other side:

What did you expect?
You, vulnerable like that, and sex-starved?

If you don't want to suffer, don't play poker
With the guy who has nothing to shuffle.

That man didn't know my little wall trick
With the dead spouse. Didn't know any of this

When I returned his utensils, his map books,
Depositing each of these things on his porch.

Reminders, they seemed, to all three of us.
I left each of them, you see, one at a time.

Why It Takes a Poet and a Private I

We are on a stakeout.
I am scrolling, reading up on Poets.org
All about the lovers Marianne Moore
Didn't have, and the flames
Robert Lowell did. The heaters in the van
Don't really work, but poems can
Steam things up
So we unroll the windows.
We sit, a pair in plain sight,
Waiting for a man who will leave
His house. Clickity snap.
Got him. My companion's camera
Shutters and my poem comes unsheathed;
Image by image, our man is caught and penned:
Surveillance for us to live by—
the two of us breathing in relief.

BARRY MCKINNON ·

Gone South

> **gone south:** This expression is generally thought to allude to compasses and two-dimensional maps where north is up and south is down. However, among some Native Americans, the term was a euphemism for dying, and possibly this sense led to the present usage.

> **(also head south, take a turn south, go south) 1 v phr** *by 1940s* To disappear; fail by or as if by vanishing [examples omitted] **2 v phr** *by 1925* To abscond with money loot, etc. [examples omitted] **3 v phr** *underworld by 1950* To cheat, esp to cheat at cards [examples omitted] 4 v phr *by 1980s* To lessen; diminish [examples omitted] Probably from the notion of disappearing south of the border, to Texas or to the Mexican border, to escape legal pursuit and responsibility; probably reinforced by the widespread Native American belief that the soul after death travels to the south, attested in American Colonial writing fr the middle 1700s; *GTT*, "Gone to Texas, absconded," is found by 1839.

in Arizona

in Arizona
the desert—weather within

weather, no discernible season, sense of its ancient

growth—the Sequoia? tree, names I don't know—the desert sans name/ or taxonomy/but for this little burst, minute, pink to cactus red buds to take as measure. (what was or is it in a temporality/does not need us nor, without a mind, need itself. thus…it's worse than the puzzle it appears.

the desert

/no matter the temperature/cold sun stings. this/no meaning as is with any sensation being only itself in the same condition.

the desert

looking at an interior, *not* yrself exactly—but a vast expanse that if you entered wld you be you? this was its fear, yr fear, all fear in whatever risk one or it takes.

•

going north in Arizona

/get back to the literal—as communication:

was in a line-up in *Basha's* with a young man ahead—as my dad once
sd—whose head fell into a tackle box: nose rings, ear rings, tattoos, skate
board pants, runners with special meanings and a toddler—not the
toddler, but he was packing a gun exposed (AZ law). my sense, to put the
grocs. down, and leave the provocation of threat and trouble. pat kid's
head. Blam! *have nice day!* Blam! whatever one cld say/taken the wrong
way.

no caring in this separation

otherwise, the bartender at the *Sultanas* in Williams Arizona stiffed me for
15 bucks.

I hesitate to say "America" in quotes when and all in all sense the largesse
unless I be taken/fooled by a more subtle commerce-training that leads to
belief of *total* sincerity.

too drunk anyway and missed Petie the dog (as *the* reason, *not* the Grand
Canyon) to see him again—100 pounds on the poolroom

table/& floor

and the quotidian 35 bucks motel, & owner Elton—and the line I use: "I
like you" as a way to disarm the possibilities of its opposite.

•

at the south end of/
the Grand Canyon, the drop/one mile down. fear starts.
I cldn't look/went
into the forest stumbling/told me nothing more than it did.
in Arizona.

•

dog minutes

"young old man"—
bent/*wrinkles.* my human dog age 10. then think

"life is like a river" (a complex flow of.../mindless
flood/over Cottonwood Island while sun's co-optive measure/melts
a long sentence that precedes its meaning/leading   to a bridge
that draws girders to let steamboats pass 100 years ago. old Fraser
      bridge—preamble
to the future—opening to what I was going to say
                    in dog years
to sense a way—release tensions of fight and flight *without* fight or
flight—a condition wielded then welded to *all* that angered me *not
forgiven! be without them!*
                    in the dog minutes ahead.

   •

tinkered w/a "poem"—& thot call it all "draft" to assume you'll never get
it, sensing then *no need to.* think: how does taking care of the *88 Buick* fit
in—or sense of love lost (when it never left? these double tangengental
thots without recourse to one's good sense and single meaning. *what
everyone dreads*

is an end

resolve? dissolve? forcing oneself to happiness—a spectre out of
the weight (of weightless thot

thinking beauty of river tree and wind in no sentimental way—a kind of
clarity without knowing but its moment.

   •

dead ends. senseless to go on to arrive at what? and then reminded/
remembered my old anxieties *not* so strong—but a preoccupation of what
you always knew *as you*—to find enough room between the ditch and
bank to turn. *more* washouts!—holes and steeper edges—some road left.

   •

the accumulation of *all* that was—*all* that did not
change. the mind when it did not *know* its future stretched/a field/to
darker clouds—when yr wordless perplexity *was* the mind as body of the
world's impending exit
to what's already gone

—the human embrace to leave who need it most

·

the old farm gone. roads re graded. foolish act to go back—to what *was*
there *there*. how to say "emptiness" in memory—in an insistence to
imagine you *were* there. fear and what makes it less: *terror of all else.* in the
Carsland bar where I used to wait. *the past* where I now await…we're all
related…leaving…

obsessive clouds to the east curved down to fields—

·

the place where memory began/*replaced*—useless to name or
describe—the past neutraled & what's ahead *the dread of what remains*

heartbreak/—its infinite distance/hope to nothing/

in harsh oppositions gain truer self & being

·

desert notebook

to see

this desert/ringed by what we sense
removes it all. yet the coagulations of its force alive as context for

its various light & range of temperatures/temperaments/—

solitude sans meaning become dust

·

(I *am* in a desert—more a field—*it's dirt*—a valley harrowed/browned/
parched—circled/mountains, distant/browned, blurred—boulders

cupped/back
drop sky/intensity/blue/

—footprints/trail/...

beauty cannot make it anything else

•

Hemet to Surprise—into high
desert—
- mindless
/the mind "undescribed" by elements that form/elements and meaning/
sun &
literal...

(*no cloud.* bush "measures" wind. dust way off to a horizon south to
Mexico, funnels.

trails "go" where...

the desert

•

what failing reveals/*makes closer*
the sun, the blanched air to shadow/textures/——& desert vectors -

these mountains folding in mute desert light?

•

the characteristic - (*suffering* humans
in relation to this basin/valley—heat bowl/persistent as
a force that rejects them—

the desert lives like water.

•

nothing becomes another thing

body in mind in context indistinguishable from what defines it
—*gone south*

ANDY MEYER

Untitled

A tree in the back
yard—ragged with
lichen like eczema—
on the top branch,
three-fingered, nipped
once by what-
ever, a chickadee
posts: ask it, from one
side of the window, why
& how you
god-damned perfectly formed
round bird, foraging
and hiding your shit, all
at once, watching
for the uglier neighbors,
loving them (or so).

Declaration(s)

We hold
these things to be

    static

as well
    (just as) as
self-evident. & just
as well, without losing

    any sleep—&
not just any sleep.

Westward Expansion

& into the night
light we go, the buzzing
neon, atomized
persona, mystified
perception, & the bus,
the forty-nine, jostling
over deconstructed brain-case-
shaking roads,
taking corners only
the conscious have thought
through, taking liberties
with all the passengers, & offering
ifs, &s, buts, & howevers
all the way, wanton. It's
a rough nite when the West
slides beneath the map,
& the map, in tow, goes too.

Lichen

Lichen loves it—
Lichen told me so.
Don't just talk to any
body along the road.
Lichen loves that too—
enough to eat
it, all done up
in slow-time drag, & awful
sweet if, lichen-like,
you think through
your teeth.

CATH MORRIS ✎

Motorless Replicant

maybe it's true
that we're nothing but cleverly programmed
giant flesh and bone robots

sometimes I feel like a motorless replicant
sometimes I feel like a motorless replicant

each one set for a specified few years
with built-in desires and emotions—
a body flying into the river—
a severed arm off on its own—
and a good working mechanism for tears

but we have composite blood
some other supra-galactic origins mixed in:

sometimes I feel like a motorless replicant
sometimes I feel like a motorless replicant
sometimes I feel like a motorless replicant
a long long way from Home

I hope it's true, Mr. Tyrell,
'cause I'd like an operation if it's so—
you can snip the wires around the heart
and set it free—like a crushed bird—

you made us too well, Mr. Tyrell,
Geneticist, Snake Charmer, Devil, Witch;
you tinkered with some tender toys
and some of the wires have got loose;

it's that persistent memory of two moons I can't shake—

and we sang like glass harmonicas in a high-pitched wail,
like heart-broken tin men in a field of monkeys…

it's that notion of a sublime,
infinitely old, infinitely wise race
that shook off its shackles millennia ago
I can't shake

and it's the high-pitched dancing of giant soft robots
in the double-helix moonlight
round a great sparkling fire
against an infinite night...

sometimes I feel like a motorless replicant
a long, long way from my star.

Somebody's Daughter

throwing caution to the wind
is alright when you're a 23-year-old wunderkind
but for us here trying to hold down the grass
it's a different matter
our greying hair pining, intertwining
vines shining

I live in Storyland alone
on the banks of Metrodome
it rushes by like rocket-sòng
but I ignore the throng

I thought you'd come
but you're so late
I'm having second thoughts
by the time you bloody get here
my sweet sad flesh will rot

so take your dear sweet time, my love
and I will all the pleasures shove
right up your dear sweet bum

while young drunken voices echo down my street
I turn to meat
did you know they're making litter out of wheat?

like smoking, laughing, joking
flipping dimes,
rhyme is the new crime
and the apoplectic pantomime continues in
the stacked parade—the big charade

and while the world gets progressively hotter
just wanted you to know
I was somebody's daughter

PETER MUNRO ✒

A Fisheries Scientist Learns to Clean Flounder

Flicking up a pectoral fin, the old man
slid his knife by. Viscera ballooned
through the brisk incision, gut-coils
splurging between his thumb and forefinger.
Startled, I snatched my glance away then forced
my eyes back, just as quickly. The dorsal fin
rippled and flinched as his edge passed through
the spinal cord. Then the head was off,
a little triangle barely wider than a knife handle.
The sudden and unknown purples,
the intestine unkinking in a slouch of pink,
and the sprawl of pyloric ceacum
all burst into a clarity that has remained
crisp after forty-seven years.

And, alive still in my hands,
I can feel how monofilament line had flaked
off my reel when I'd sounded the shallows with bait,
plunking sinker and hook down the four fathoms
of salt-chuck under the old man's dock.

I do not remember his face or his name,
the gentleman who showed me the proper way.
Kneeling on his timber planks, we gutted
above the shadows that had produced
my catch of meager flatfish.
He reached in from beside my vision, the skin
on the backs of his hands wrinkled and veined,
his hands quick with practice, and, also, somehow,
kind. He paused
when I needed to see
just how my blade should go,
small spatters of flounder blood
cast across his knuckles.

Dumping Bait Bags after a Soak

Fulmars clatter and bicker,
paddling hard just abaft the shit chute,
scrabbling old bait,
the leached-out chunks of herring
no longer tarred with the stink and oils
needed to create a scent plume
that draws cod up-current.
Hooked beaks rip at the surface.
The birds' chipped-stone chitter soothes me.
I can't explain.
I cannot speak
what happens to me
when fulmars' bitter competition erupts
and bullet-sleek birds zoom to our flank
to gash the sea ragged. Words don't work,
too long leached of a reek sufficient to the task,
no longer gravid or fecund
or even loaded with stink,
exhausted from overlong soaks.

If one launches gear along a brink,
lays out pots in a string where the shelf
breaks to abyss,
and if scattered, nameless fish
glimmer up from the black
like blue flame finning into invisible wind,
flickering as they follow the scent plume
up the continental slope,
and if the photophores burning cold
in their skins illuminate the bait's faint messages
raveled downstream in diaspora,
molecules received perfectly into long-evolved
sensory pores, then expect miracle.

Except such fishes never come.
I wait upon Mystery.
I catch only cod.
Fulmars hurtle crosswind to pluck discard
dumped like so much doxology and laud.

How the Spirit Drives Music through the Body

1   Night In Tunisia

When she pumps her trumpet-bellows,
he hits a note higher than delight.
His mouthpiece burns. He would swallow
spit but the embouchure of the night
opens to receive those tallows
which he blows out then reignites
measure after measure of the wind
she drives across vibrating skin.

2   Miles Runs The Voodoo Down

He has never flexed that muscle
she fingers to sparkle her grace notes.
He shoves melody through gristle,
spit, and wind, composing by rote
ligament to his bitch's whistle.
She forces her tunes from his throat.
His lips ache and his breath runs thin,
bending under her load of din.

3   West End Blues

He'd smoked so many cigarettes
her wind switched from southerly to north.
Now knife-work bloodies lazarets
and abattoirs chill minor mirths.
He scats the Muggles Minuet.
His lover trumpets a harlot's worth.
By glory hole, the whoremother
gales him up to kiss the Other.

4   Concerto For Cootie

She likes it low, deep and dirty.
She takes it down into the guts.
Gruffly, he plunges the gritty,
rough as rage unstuffed. The man struts.
She growls, kissing without pity,
her breath in his flesh, hot as a slut's.
His mute opens, wowing slowly.
She spreads him wide for the Holy.

5   Work Song

She gusts the same through both brothers
and he knows it. He feels her at work.
But if his lover loved another
more than him, he'd labor through murk
just the same, brass-bright, unsmothered
breath filling him full as an ark.
Spilling wind into her clamor,
he beats flame, his tongue the hammer.

AMBER NELSON ✎

Coarse (The Populace You See In)

sail frothing you are forward, wind-
propelled, thinking how all of this
could mean nothing on the streets
bodies of cars, bodies of pigeons—
their toes gnarled by telephone wires
into rough-scaled doorknobs
and electric cables, bodies of people
the burning of a thousand thoughts
dressed in clothes with headphones
the whisperings of various jays in their ears
their eyes down turned on residential sidewalks
amidst the wrought iron and brick and stucco
you look in windows to find the glare
bright lights a sun to avert your eyes to the shine
of a big screen and a cat hunting squirrels
and the oily feathers of crows they dream in their teeth
through the window through the window
you almost see a life maybe a photograph
a nitrate bust a silver sliver an idea
on the wall you can't quite make out,
or a plant dangling greenly in the window
balconies and porches full of BBQ grills,
chained up bicycles, lawn chairs, strings
of out-of-season Christmas lights in one window
sometimes, when you look in the window,
you see a man standing there
looking out you see each other
for just a moment
and then you look away

Awake at First Light

                         Sometimes,
a Flicker, a bird sound—

tells us the weather
patterns, changing.

Some white blinds
            the way the sun
has done.

And I feel the air
just so
everywhere.

Here, we can count
on rain
in any season. We can count

the times we see blue.

But we cannot count
the words it takes
to make it so.

            This is all to say
it's spring—and that whole
cities have been born

one day, with wildflowers.

There will be no more
words, at the end. I will

have no more words.
At the end, there will be no more—

30. The Day the Weather Decided to Die

(After a Haida tale told by Robert Bringhurst)

> *On hearing the wooden rumble of thunder we realize that we are
> situated below the platform of the sky.* –Ramón Gomez de la Serna

What constitutes a good family they say and give instructions to servants
under the backdrop of the hugest sucking sound in history prelude to when
the wind'd no longer rumble from under the skirt of the great Ma no longer
float a blue heron's Xacho-side lumber no longer sustain.

Age of celebrity
tattoo news, of the rise of Yurok Duwamish Tsimshian Haida Puyallup
Muckleshoot Musqueam of tornadoes hurricanes earthquakes tsunamis
bee silence Fukushima and Fukushimas to come.

The weather born out
of cockleshell embryo or out of snot, weather that hunts birds and sends
winds out in the skins of blue jay, weather that steals hats of campesinos
(compassions) for kicks, weather that would sprout houses when adopted by
a master carver, weather that would be a scholar of carving.

The weather when
painted would sit facing the sea would weep for owls with spots and the new
northward range of dolphin's neighborhood weather that would warn of the
Big Ones who think of biting weather whose big fish story is dried halibut
and waits and waits and waits for a shift in settler rituals.

It could start with
today is a good day to die could start with the inheritance of the campesino
(compression) who opened up about his daily prayers for humility or when
he the one born in a cockleshell wd dress as wren & sit way above the sea as
a cumulus cloud waiting to see what his latihan would bring: dance, song,
chant or something more cathartic just beyond his out-stretched wings.

Remember: crow's yr brother, stumps
never lie, we
hold up the sky.

Juan Vicente de Güemes Padilla Horcasitas y Aguayo, 2nd Count of Revillagigedo

y who is de *San Juan* after whom
              de islas de San Juan are named?
              & how did Spaniards

    get here and who, why, how
                   did the blood stop
          at one pig, how
                were the war pigs (for once)
                                      denied
                                      (denuded

divested of covering
made bare?)

                          Coulda been war, glorious
                              here in *Isla y Archiepelago de San Juan.*

                    Cannon balls and musket blasts
        to scatter the last of the Canis lupis
                      the Columbia Black-Tailed Deer, the
                      rare Northern Sea Otter (for whom

      or whose pelt Quimper would trade copper
      years before Filthy Jerry cd get his
                filthy fingers on it.)

But there's something in the Cascadia water wd
                        bring out the noble in men
              like Admiral Baynes who'd soon
                            be knighted
              who'd refuse Governor Douglas'
                      August 2, 1859, troop landing order.

          Something that'd attract
                    Spaniards like the Mexican Viceroy:

Juan Vicente de Güemes Padilla Horcasitas y Aguayo, 2nd Count of
Revillagigedo

(Not the San Juan who'd be put in a cell not much bigger than himself. Not the one who'd see the union of jiwa and Divine in the metaphor of Holy Marriage. Not the one who'd write about how the bride hides herself and abandoned him in his lonely groaning. Not the one who'd feel the need to purge every last imperfection every last psychic typo every last lust urge every last of the dominator fixation not mitigated but transcended by The Fire to which Blaser wd allude. Not the he of a thousand graces diffusing, graces unnumbered, those that protect from the thousand cuts that come from conceptions of the Beloved. Not the one whose metaphor'd bride'd leave his heart there in that lashed meat cage maintained by a bit of bread and salted fish. Not the one with the silvered surface who'd one day mirror forth. Not the one on the wing whose Beloved'd one day see the strange islands with the roaring torrents (Cascade Falls?) & whose gales would whisper amour, a love-awakening south wind not spewed by Spetsx who'd be the rain wind from the Southwest a two day canoe journey south of the present scene. Not the one whose Beloved bride from a mother corrupted would make a bed out of flowers, protected by lions hung with purple and crowned with a thousand shields of gold. Not the one whose bride'd attract young ones & who'd commence the flow of divine balsam & get him pitchdrunk on fire and scent and spiced wine. Not he of all consuming painless fire drunk on pomegranate wine whose only job was amour. Not that San Juan.)

This Juan was a Cubano,
　　　　born in La Habana.
　　　　　　The third Criollo Viceroy
　　　　　　　　of Hispaña Nueva.

This Juan wd see
　　　　the Capital (then Veracruz)
　　　　　　　　as a slum, peasants
　　　　　　in thin robes, straw hats, trash
　　　　　　in the streets and the first flash
　　　of all those Rez dogs to come.

　　　　　　　　　　This Juan
(el Vengador de la Justicia)
　　　　　　he'd find & hang
　　　　　　the outlaw gangs
　　　　　　　　of murderers

& clean the Viceroy's palace.

Light the streets of Ciudad de México
pave highways to Veracruz,
                    Acapulco,
                    Guadalajara,
                    San Blas y
                    Toluca

find the Aztec Calendar Stone & set
    the heavens on fire but found
            Cascadia

                        not worth the troops
    it'd cost to own her,
                settled
                        for leading the flock
        of 4.5 million future Mexicans
                        he'd count and a few islands
        to this day
                in one way or another
                        bear his name:

San Juan
            Orcas
                Guemes.

Dots in a green landscape
            as seen from Constitution
                    where the divine balsam flows
            by the kayaks
                    and the wind whispers

            Mary.

DOUG NUFER ☙

from **"The Me Theme"**

Just ice justice, reinstate rein
State the me theme
Factor fact or temper
A mental temperamental
Leg end legend.

Mistrust mist, rust art if ice,
Artifice restrains rest
Rains beat.

Be at bat on baton
Wag on wagon auto mated car, a van
Automated caravan assembling
As sembling per uses
Illiterate peruses.

I'll iterate the me theme
Just ices justice's den.

I, Zen denizen,
Am using amusing cons
Trained constrained
Imbedding I'm bedding.

Polyphilia is on
Polyp hi liaison,
A basing abasing
Onsets on sets.

I'm a gist imagist
A polo gist apologist, a
Bashed abashed agent, a gent
Attesting at testing
Artichoke art
I choke
Anthems, ant hems

Poe try poetry
Port rayed portrayed temperas
Temp eras formats for mats.
Rampages ramp ages ram pages.

*

Yakima yak? I'm a Tacoma taco Ma, yum.
A Yuma par is Paris sand
I, ego San Diego, tamp.

A Tampa Rom a Roma bar
Row Barrow tor
On to Toronto.

Pensacola pens a cola
Or leans Orleans wall a wall a Walla Walla
Victoria victor.

I, a Marin mar in re: no Reno
Nor folk Norfolk
Stock ton Stockton day ton
A Daytona C-level and Cleveland
Cash mere Cashmere red ding.

Redding band on Bandon reed
Sport Reedsport Logan log
An Elma elm a belling ham Bellingham.

Chic ago, Chicago ran goon Rangoon crime;
A Crimea Jackson jacks on war
Saw Warsaw tole do Toledo mad
Rid Madrid, man a squan Manasquan son
Or a Sonora Manhattan man hat
An Athens at hens washing ton Washington bud
A pest Budapest Dunedin dune din sing a pore Singapore
As wan Aswan Hanoi?

Ha, no I be I
Rut Beirut, nag a saki
Nagasaki rotter, dam Rotterdam liver,
Pool Liverpool bright on Brighton.
Tunis tun is my sore Mysore Pullman pull man Galway gal way
Bangalore, ban gal ore bang a lore ban galore.

JOHN OLSON ✒

Smart and Black and Full of Birds

There can be no mistaking it: I write poetry for the delirium.
Thought is reflective, quiet, that's not it, not what a poem is, not
entirely. It's too wild, too eccentric, spinning out of control. It's
flashy and ridiculous like an amusement park ride. Lights flashing
people screaming. I want a hat like that. I want a hat ringed with
flashing bulbs. A marquee hat. A hat that bridges dream and reality.
A hat that describes life as a difficulty so entirely palpable it tastes
of bells. Something mechanical, a machinery of words, a rattling of
bolts and screws, consciousness unzipped and obscene. Something
immodestly aquatic. A hat like that. Delinquent and wax and scarlet
and warm. Pickled in calculus. Glissandos around the brim. Maybe
a Cubist comb or two stuck in the band, which will be a band like
the Beatles, no leather band, no silk band, no sireee, A Hard Day's
Night band, a henna band, a Hannah Arendt band, a crease on
top, and dipped in Keats. I want to traipse around with the music
of helium on my head. Contemptuous and desperate and full of
graceful articulation. I'm not kidding. I'm not being ironic. What am
I saying? I'm being very ironic. I'm being so ironic I can't but help
being sincere. I can be sincerely insincere but I cannot be insincerely
sincere. It's not in me. And I don't have the right kind of hat. That
would take a very different kind of hat. An ironic hat. A snarky hat.
Fuck that hat. I'm wearing this hat. This is the hat for me. The hat
of experience. The hat of exotic tinctures. A Colorado hat. A Rocky
Mountain hat. A hat crowned with snow. The kind of hat Charles
Baudelaire would wear. Smart and black and full of birds.

And What

One must think radically in order to break a habit. Some habits are better left alone. One has to ask oneself: is this a habit I can live with? If it is the habit of writing, then yes. I can live with that. Does the world want me to write? The world doesn't give a shit about anything I do. And isn't that pretty much everyone's situation?

And isn't it funny that when I say 'world,' we know what is meant by world. And when I say we 'we' know what is meant by we.

Though I can already hear someone out there saying no. I don't know what you mean by 'world.' I don't know what you mean by 'we.' And fuck you.

And who can blame them? Who doesn't like fucking?

Here is a list of twenty things I like:

1. *The Sadness of the King,* by Henri Matisse.
2. Dark chocolate cordial cherries.
3. *Finnegans Wake,* by James Joyce.
4. *Meat Science Essays,* by Michael McClure.
5. Spoons.
6. Hardware stores.
7. Toby in his paper fort looking out on the world as if from a secret place.
8. Anything surprising and unpredictable (provided that it results in something good and not something bad, like a flat tire, or a fart when bowing to the Queen of England).
9. A nice warm shower after running five miles on a winter afternoon.
10. Metaphors.
11. "The Bees Made Honey in the Lion's Skull," Earth.
12. "The Wicked Messenger," the Dylan song covered by the Black Keys.
13. "Algiers," by the Afghan Whigs.
14. "Gimme Something Good," by Ryan Adams.
15. "Eine Kleine Nachtmusik" by Amadeus Mozart.
16. Waterfalls.
17. Rumination.
18. Formulas. Just the idea of formulas. But especially the formula for cough syrup with codeine.
19. Cows.
20. Crows

And what? What else? Pink. Pink is a crucial color. Though not as crucial as black. I can't explain black. What makes black so compelling? What makes black such an interesting climate? Because the stars shine out of it? Because old men play concertinas on darkly lit Montmartre streets? Because white is so freakishly weird and scary? Because bleak yet starkly beautiful places like the Antarctic are redeemed by black rocks and penguins?

In a word, yes. And the crunch and rusted nails and rotting timber of fantasy ships. Baudelaire's albatross aloft once again, and the sun dropping handsprings of light on the ice, where it gleams, gleams terribly, hurting the eyes, until the night arrives bloated and blissful and black.

And all those stars up there shining out of that black making you dizzy with infinity. And you wonder how something comes out of nothing. And how can nothing exist if there isn't something to make nothing nothing? There can be no nothing if there isn't something. No something, no nothing. So is nothing something? The soft dominion of snow is a kind of answer. The ice glistens saying something else. The semantic glistening of ice fulfills the glimmering abyss of the infinite and the elegant pain of inscrutability that accompanies the burning wind. The ice says cold. The ice says move, or freeze. And you move. And the skin gets twisted into another day of exploration and the search for imponderable answers and you know that death is real and no one gets out alive but because of habit which is a funny engine fueled by the basal ganglia, things that need getting done get done.

Mechanical or artfully it all gets done. Even as we daydream, lose ourselves in reverie, the body knows what to do, and we arrive at our destination or sit down to a plate of pancakes.

Habits are funny. They're the little narratives that structure that flimsy overlook protruding over the abyss.

Everything else is proclivity. Mindfulness, seed, and serendipity.

Sock

There's a pretty density which grips a sock, makes it a sock, socks it into sockness, soaks it in the energy of sensation and parachutes it through oblivion. This is the reality of the sock. The quiet weave of the sock is its unity, a continuous union as in association and thinking. If the phenomenon of the sock is established through the form of time, then the phenomenon that is consciousness is a unifying activity. We see that the relationship between consciousness and the sock represents a transcendent, unchanging reality apart from time. The life of an individual is the development of consciousness that constitutes a sock. But which sock? For there is a left sock and a right sock. The right sock is independent of the left sock and the left sock is independent of the right sock. For when one sock is lost in the laundry the other sock loses the penetrating force of its utility and becomes a rag-like thing whose only saving feature is that it may join forces with another sock, a sock that it may or may not match imperfectly, or with enough conviction that it may pass as the other sock's true mate. There is always a certain unchanging reality at the base of the sock. This reality enlarges from day to day until it develops a hole and a toe pokes through. This is the reality of the toe in conjunction with the reality of the sock. One might wonder about its form and how it maintains itself. The form of the toe and the form of the sock form a conjunction by which the hole itself becomes an entity, a hollowness whose integrity comes from an absence of material, acrylic or cotton worn down until it is nothing, and a toe appears, that is the fundamental fact emerging from another reality. All people believe that there is a fixed, unchanging principle in the universe and that all things are established according to it. This principle is the sock that unifies consciousness. It is not possessed by mind or matter but establishes them. There, in the laundry basket, or upon one's foot, tugged into place, toe poking through, where it is an object of consciousness, a cotton or acrylic form occupying a certain time in a certain place, and may be regarded as singular, however imperfectly it matches the other sock, the other lost sock, given a place at the extremity of one's leg, joined together by linguistic signs, by words, these words, which I have offered to fill the sock, and make the sock a sock, and not just the word of the sock, but the sock itself, as I sock it to you.

CATHERINE OWEN ✒

Last Request

I want to fall asleep with the black rhino as it becomes extinct
Between the heated sand sheets of some lonely Serengetial bed

& slumber in the ice caves of Everest with the people who lay
Down on the mountain's final silk and did not wake,

Becoming effigies of preparation in their eternity of snowsuits
& silence.

Yes, I want to rest with them now, curl like he did before he died,
His bony alphabet of limbs folded close, and relinquish

What I cannot lose again, and there will be the slow purl
When breathing descends on its mercury and I will

Watch the vanishing & frozen & his memory as dream's
Whole darkness nurseries us—yes, that desire.

In Homage to Charles Wright

January, early on.
          What animal-year is this?
Either way, a sunrise lifts the river to my seeing & I am a reverse

        Li Po of joy. Sunfish razzling the log booms.
One heron erasing all those engines.

      Darkness coming later again,
        then later.

*

Can't speak of a god. Won't. Something, he says,
      may Something await me.
Glenn, macular degeneration weeping his eyes to milk, 84, pouring

          with stories, has a word, each night, with the dark
possibility he will be saved before death
      from dying. Nothing answers.

The hummingbird feeder has been moved inside the house.
      Mist froths over the pond; turns glass.
Thinking one should write an elegy for the world is not the same thing

             as being commissioned to.

*

Poetry, to most, is cuckoo clocks: retro, niche, tacky, invisible. Who knows.

    But not what we feel it to be. The ache-pulse of the essential saying itself.
Singing really. A score for the lovely darkness. Crows on each stave.

Reading Jeffers,
Merwin,
Wright,

I need no savior.

      The sky a perfect gospel; earth a recurrent homily.

January. Still at the beginning.

    What can steal me from myself now.

SHIN YU PAI ☙

Bell (e)

(after Toshiko Takaezu)

in centuries
past, sunk
beneath soil

to draw earth's
vital force, inert
vessel of

sound + light,
conserved

in a museum
of curative plants
the moment of

stillness &
gathering before
the shudder

of first sound

dreaming
the shake of chime,
hum &

g o n g

Iron Chink

when E.A. Smith failed
to collect a return on his
investment due to labor

issues at the Chilcat
cannery, he took matters
into his own hands

to build a machine
better than any Chinese

laborer it had to butcher
more piles of sockeye &

salmon then a Chinaman
could process by hand alone

in a ten-hour shift more
than two thousand fish

still not fast enough

to turn a profit
blood up to their

waists, wading
through carpets

ten feet long,
a forty-foot spread

the slitters cut off
heads & fins, slit

open the belly
slimers gutted,

cleaning the cavity,
removing the scales

so choppers could
slice the fish into steaks

the length of cans
fillers, wipers & cappers

finished off

by a machine its
inventor coined

the iron chink,
the "Perfect Fish Cleaning

Machine" developed to
stamp out the need for
so many hired
hands, butchers,
migrant workers

living hand to mouth

self-park

condensation   fogging   windshields   is   one   sure   tell-tale
sign,   towels   pinned   over   windows,   rusted   trucks   crowded   full
of   plastic   bags   of   shit,   hippy   family   packed   into   a   van   rock
a   newborn   infant   fast   asleep,   officers   mark   car   windows   with
this   day's   date,   a   woman   stows   her   cat's   ashes   beneath
a   seat,   the   cost   of   gas   crests   again,   still   one   paycheck   away   from
the   street,   in   the   fifth   year   of   the   city's   master   plan   to   eradicate
homelessness—an encampment of wagons sprawled beneath the interstate

JEREMY PATAKY

Aural

We were all on time, once
hunkered in the medians

attuned to the addled clamor
where we built our nests.

No need to make
attempts on some new world

no cause for forward thinking.
And if the sound of lifting jets

eclipses the false noise of traffic
give up all listening and let the sounds

hemorrhage into whatever memories
of natural quiet you can find,

unbidden as a memory of taste
or a scent wafting into a sleep

your first rain on your first roof
calling birds muted by the river in flood.

Anthropocene

Landed, calm, look back:
what mappers of water devised a life like this?
The landscape's voice is liquid, even under
the report of rocks colliding, the calls of birds,
and the rare lightning.

The light outdoes itself,
destroys shame and love and envy
for the possibilities of light.
All the while, rain
and the sound of rain disperses into clear, cold air
and the sounds of the two swollen creeks talk a robins-egg blue
out of ice, talk a sky blue back to sky between clouds, with chords,
talk the color white into the falling water too distant to be heard.
It does sing. I hear the flow nearby sing its way
under the flared wing of the glacier, tired of migrating,
glacier far from the sea, glacier of the anthropocene.

It cracks its back, busts our skin, holds us back,
and describes thrill rides of long descents down the icefall.
I am miles and days from home and I smell home
in this post-rain fragrance of cold air settled from the alpine
and wafted down in busy katabatics.

The dual work of this creek will sew shut
the dark evening, blue and mauve, peregrine,
olive and amethyst, snowberry amid grays
all sorting themselves out before me
where my only ambitions involve a few more minutes here
before lying down to fall, not far, to sleep.

Steeped

Outside the cabin, black rain
runs into a glass rainbow,
an actual one lighting
an actual willow bush
already turned yellow inside
the still-green forest.
I think I'll never leave
and in staying I will
drink a lifetime's worth
of the kind creek. I say
I'll meet you in town
in one month
and we'll eat dinner.
Two thousand miles
down the coast,
a black bear swims
to a beach on an island
capped with a house
and bites holes in a rubber
Zodiac that deflates
as the sun comes up.
The family, asleep inside,
is stranded, and the animal
is gone when they wake.

Inside my cabin,
I boil rainwater for tea
and listen to the birdless quiet
as leaves steep and slabs of color
bleed back into the wet light.

CHARLES POTTS ❧

Beginning with a Line by Robert Duncan

for Edward Smith

"Often I am permitted to return to a meadow"
My horses have eaten all the handy grass off of
By late August so I supplement them with a little alfalfa
Salt and minerals staring into autumn overlooked by
Indifferent Douglas Fir and Yellow Pine
Nearby to the cliff across Blue Creek
Where mountain spring water flows down a moss frond
To fill my mouth, my *Body's Many Cries for Water*
As the Iranian doctor Batmanghelidj put it
Out of my mind, into my element, keeping time to an insatiable rhythm:
All things can happen to you if you live long enough.

I've lived long enough with the sorrowful empire
In a village preoccupied by geriatric republicans
Who have enough votes for a new cop shop
A new fire station, and a few years before
A new juvenile detention center
But not enough for a swimming pool
Sunk in the retail advertising that passes for news
Worshipping security seething with hatred of youth.

Did I mention the colonial wars ad infinitum
Prosecuted by paranoids too saturated with fear
Feigning reluctance and scooping up no-bid contracts
To notice that they with their sixteen separate spy agencies
Are the most significant threat
To peace on earth in their perpetual practice of war.

I'm an old man
Once a youth
Many old friends dead
My wife dead
My dying dreams fade by the wayside.

The lovely shadows of the black locust dance
In the breeze on this yellow legal pad.

Twice now colts of mine have been clawed up by cougars:
Quanah in June and Frosty in August.
I come back with a 30:06
Not wanting to return to Burlingame Meadow
And my homemade corral
To find
A dead horse only four months young devoured in
The predatory teeth of a mountain lion
When I was not there to
Stop such natural nonsense.

When I return to the meadow and find them alive
Anxiety bursts into calm
Feeling obliged to return to the meadow
Obligated not merely permitted
To defend my horses
To remind them of our binding
Herd with a human leader
I groom them, feed them, trim their feet
Dreaming of them, worrying about them
More them than me as their eyes
Take me in
Far from any other people
In the insect silence of the meadow.

The Task Master

Your job
Makes no difference
Whether or not you accept it
Avoid getting hit by falling pieces of the empire.

C.E. PUTNAM ☙

DAY 22
FIRST, THIS TREE IS EASY TO CLIMB

In no time at all the smoke
mangoes had been eaten.
I put a silver penny
in the music box.
A large insect-o-freak
antennae growing through
the fourth floor
window frame.
Midtown incinerators
blacken the new
fallen snow with
Styrofoam ash.

Yowling hounds get kissey
after a second bowl
of mimosa. The yellow
orange flesh browns
and sours. I spit out
red plastic bags.

I want to eat a wolf
but I'm afraid this will change
me. A trail of roach
droppings now over my legs
how did I get this
paralyzed—twitching
a panicked creature bumping
against the lid of the boil pot
or lawn mowers running
loose in a freshly
buried casket.
Does your belly bear
the mark of the six stars?

No one really knows about
my absolute hunger
since my diagnosis
a small sweet lick of the underbelly
can feed my music machine.

Green tambourine
I just want to
watch my life go
by undisturbed.

DAY 123
KISS ME LUCILLE ALOHA SKELETON ALOHA

Yak handler Ken grabbed the reins
again, his ghost horse foaming up
at me inside the buffalo box car I now
call my home. By nightfall, the horse
was buried in the falling crematorium
snow. The Mice set up the gambling
board and began to play among the grey
flakes. Through a knothole, I saw a field
that had just been burned by farmers
to clear and enrich the soil. An awful
feeling to visually understand. It looks
like it's starting to rain. "I am not yet
strong enough to resist her," Ken said.
He climbed a tree and poked himself
in the eye. "I want to be just like YOU."
This, Lucille Aloha Skeleton did. She sat
down on my radius. Left me cold. Lucille
has no suffering herself, but spreads
it around through song. He carried her
into his hut and made a fire to dry
her off and warm her up. He goes
with the yaks whenever they wander
at night and even when he cases
something fine he doesn't go out
of their sight. When he returned
that evening his horse had left
only an ashless shadow behind.

He was humming drunk in a river
of fire, the wood hut now cracking
and smoke choked. The warning
present is a compliment above
the breast plate. It is her best song:
her sweet skin dreaming without bones.

DAY 164
BEFORE YOU PUT IT IN THE PAN

Ministry Majesty Ministry says:

The citizen's only power can only be realized through…

But I stop listening and think

     spanking red tofu
     don't fight it
     27 times I think
     don't fight it
     spanking red tofu

DAY 292
THE STARFISH AND THE SEA URCHIN LISTEN
TO THE SEA-CUCUMBER'S SONG

        The light the shine inside
        it says the shine inside
        the light it says the fire
        inside the fire it says the smoke
        the air it rings it says the dark
        tastes its flesh it says
        drawing in the dead light
        it says into a throbbing
        maw it says the floor
        is sand and bones it says
        and when the shine is gone
        it says it's then the shadows
        go it says it's then the
        shadows go it says.

MEREDITH QUARTERMAIN ✎

Canada

This is why we drive, why we celebrate, why the worst bullying happens in groups, and why we stand on borders, we yawn, say eh, why we do statistics and grow horses. This is why we need government, we do assessments and workouts, Royal Commissions, we bother, eat donuts, why we brag about winter, do broadcasts, play hockey. This is why we eat cod-liver oil and back-bacon, why we sweep ice, call it cultural capital. Why route rhymes with boot and not clout. Why we grow 8 million hectares of wheat and play baseball, we make domestic products, die of cancer and heart attacks instead of bombs or famine. Why our sea-to-sea store sells tires, we don't spell perimeter like metre or honour like motor. This is why we sell oil and gas, not coffee or computers, why we have armed services and forestry, armorial bearings, the fur trade, parties and ice-breakers. Why we have maple syrup, lions holding maple leaves, we have occupations and food-rules, we go into space with unicorns waving fleurs-de-lis. It's why we work like beavers, not eagles, chew and dam on average 10 hours a week for personal care, which is why we tattoo ourselves, deke out of kerfuffles, get pissed about ridings. Why we put rubbers on our feet. It's why anglophones telephone francophones. This is why we drive clicks, not mphs, wearing tuques on our zeds and toonies on our cheques. It's why we have freight-rates and margarine wars, why police ride steeds, we eat 175 kilos of veg a year and potatoes are veg, trans is a highway or a fat. We can send a letter one click or 6000 for half a loonie which is or isn't crazy for selves at odds with our brains.

Invention 36

A boutique where you try on Mum's *Don't tell me* or Dad's *bamboozle*. Grandpa's *Howdy doody*, Grandma's *Good gracious*.

Try on skin. White. Black. Gold. Or sheer. A transparent handbag. Through which intestines coiling. Heart pulsing. Blood running.

Replace intestines with soil. Heart with molten magma. Blood with bacterial telephone lines.

Here, use the undressing room. My misfitifier will show you all the latest metasuits and matchistic snugitude for concrete walls, boardrooms and parties. Antivisibility's invisible. Its space-suit of silver windows hugs your shape.

Step into my mirrored room, turn around, turn inside out. Mirrors within mirrors disappear in this little transparency handbag. And while you're in there caper about, do anything you want: murder a tyrant, create a cure for human cruelty.

What outfit will you choose for birth and death, love and grief? I'll measure your inside seams and crotches.

Heat Haze

Hills heads say. Hills hands hold. Hills hug. Hills hostage. They hang.
Hundreds of hills hand dull. Huging. Dullarding. Hills holed up. Old
eroded odours doldrums ponder horizon. Roads they row. Rows they
Romeo, rows they rubáiyát, they rube, roads of ruins, of rules, rods of
rudes, dunes jugged smudged muddle. They buzzard. The hills mongrel.
Dull jugs of mudded clouds moan monu-mood. The dun hills hunge over
haggard gullies. Gaze gooey. Greedy. Hill heavy. Heave vee. They hang-dog
hum mid. The hills gradual glue. Megalo bung. They midden mod-bulls
mod duels. Megalo blued booms. They haggle. Hand bond to head. Bed to
mumber. Mono gaga to molybdenum.

Old eroded hills arrange. Arraign, they say, array. We want arraigning. Play
our faces. Lathe our longwave lupine faint faded faze. These our ranges,
our mundane labours braided daze unable us, unlake us, unladel us in
caged muscle. Assail us in layers lately sliced flanges. File our irons. Untied
we wait, we old eroded tired whales. We make brigades line up our lions,
our lagging luggard lions to file. Five of them stoop and rake ruins flake
and fail. Stoop pad, stoop pud. River ground. Tired whale fire. We muggle
ground-weary baleful sluggishness corroded old draggy gauges.

Us drones the recondite information highway. Us woolgathers rabbit/
gopher this whirring transportation monotony ribbon. Interpretational
thistle ideation trucks us pensivelessness. Essential expresswayed. Us
transcendental vague quintessential coyote.

Clouds

I thought about clouds and earth. Electricities hold each other prisoner.
I thought fondly and fallen. That touching the earth is fog. Entangled
business—no, not business—yes, busyness. Last summer uncloudedly
happy for an Italian frieze. I thought about night visitors to cloudberries.
Puffs of ice cream and tower blocks. I thought in disgrace, in secrecy,
unknowingly. My flock straying west or east grazed episodically the
movement of history's saturated conditions all grey and cozy and
introverts insided. Molecules of mind jam a cloud with coherence. You
can't hold a cloud in your pocket, stuff it in a plastic bag or suitcase but
between thumb and middle finger, I thought, opens a lake and Cloud
Island directly in its mouth. I thought of OE clud a rocky hill ripening
on the female cloudberry. I wandered lonely as, and under a. Billowing.
Rapidly deepening surface. The higher the turbidity the more scattering
and densely boisterous. I thought, my flock shall not want for smudged
horizons hung over forageable prospects. You can pick cloudberries
when they're still hard, I thought, and store them under water. Millions of
thoughts deluge the clouder. Thoughts opposite charges top and bottom
browse the field's static textures. Clear weather to the stables where horses
come to work, eat a cloud or two and carrots float in blue and birds and
cats.

Dear Mom,

I've given birth to a tree and so at last you are a grandmother, and one day you'll be the great great great grandmother of a forest. How did I get pregnant with a tree, Mom. Was it from eating apple seeds? From climbing cedars? From drinking birch sap? Picking chestnuts, walnuts, hazelnuts. Carving my hearts in the oaks. I ate so many cherries and coconuts. From countless branches I hung by my knees. I think I'll never see a city lovely as my tree. Dear Mom, remember that windy-eyed man who gave you a silver snake. He's been knocking on my door. He offered me some inklings, smarts and know-hows. If he gave them to me, I had to promise to give something to him. I said No to his smarts. Then he offered me the latest most modern here-and-nows hot off the press, if only I would give this thing to him. No to your prestos, I said. I don't need your kitchen sink. Then how about a pack of trumpcards, a universal linchpin, all the keynotes and cruxes in the world and you the muscle queen, you the dominion diva. What do I want with your pullery, your cloutish aphrodisiac, I said, I have my little tree—Merrythought. Willy nilly bodacious. Willy nilly lexiludic. Biblio-baobab, my wishbone. Dear Mom, I pray no bonsai pots come near my tree. No nursery rows. No sidewalk holes. No rubber-tappers. No farming lumberjacks. Droogish oafs, oxters or boojums.

DAN RAPHAEL ✎

Moments from the History of Rain

rain wasn't always like it is now:
instead of falling it came from a hidden dimension
bringing wet the soil would welcome, wet we'd try to collect & shape

<><><>

once rain swarmed like bees, inundating fields or
selectively touching only blue collars, only animals with stubby tails.
hurricanes and tornadoes were rituals where the queen took over the sky
with unexplainable presence

<><><>

air so rich with oxygen the rain became acidic, turning giant ferns to mush,
eating away dinosaurs skins to polish their bones

<><><>

when the moon couldn't yet pull the oceans but focused the moisture exchange,
creating deficits & surpluses, hoping the right amount in the right place
would distract gravity
           wind was meatier then, strumming lunar strings,
drinking lustily yet never letting go, a river spewing its own tail.
when during summer water got so thick & redolent
we cultivated plants that hid the smells, silenced what we couldn't decide
were myths, history or infomercials

<><><>

noah's rain was 40 days and nights of drop-shaped vessels evacuating earth,
darkening the skies with all the buildings and records they destroyed—
what we thought volcanos were camouflaged incinerators

<><><>

when I come back rains at its best—unpredictable, generous & nourishing.

we still have roofs and slickers to keep from overdosing;
indoors we're naked out of reverence, deeply joyed
when our cupped hands fill with rain from elsewhere

Isthmus

you can see a million miles tonight,
but you can't get very far.
—Counting Crows

when the ocean jumps against the rock, is transformed white & leaps further
a thousand structures moved through and gone quicker than gravity.
taking a single color through all its saturations and lightsources

><><><><

this trees 5 times older than me and moves exponentially slower,
I could sit here six hours and be less than an extra needle, the unequal
    distribution of bird bombs.
how sooner or later every lost feather bursts into flame and reminds
    everyone of a different meal:
I feel the napkin tucked under my chin, the 19-year-old instep gliding along
    my ankle

><><><><

we want, we cant, we nibble away, skin always falling from us,
my brain rippling the occasional emotion as if from the outside,
more than blowing a kiss or an opportunity, belaying,
lowing like a cow instantly aware of her limits,
forgetting the robot calves she feeds twice a day who will free her

><><><><

around we are, like one continuous global coastline—
if we string all our intestines together how long till our mouths realize.
that day everyone who commuted to manhattan never came back,
the island floating a little lower, more empty shelves,
buildings sprouting extra stories overnight, sending out electrons
like micro-gulls whove lost the ability to navigate, lost the stamina,
cant sleep without falling, dont know which clouds will rain meat

><><><><

how if you took all my skin off I'd be a different form of human,
without that vibratory shield
without the accumulation of living at the frequency of meat,
how even a small cut begins to send me to another dimension,
where my wound pulls plasma from the air,
as I'm dozens of intentions bound by skin, plumbing and mutual needs.

><><><><

the time it takes a cliffside to rotate 45 degrees brings questions about
                    eggs, tensile strength, fluid dynamics,
how Ive honed my willpower to spatula strength—
the egg about to flip should ripple like a wave with a sea lion as the yolk,
foam thickening around it like a jellyfish convention,
like a large sail whipped into the sea 40 years ago evolving
its manta ray hungers,
its handholds for hitchhikers, cultures between its sheets

JAMIE REID ☙

Fake Poem 1

The last day was easy i needed to talk i needed to talk it slipped out of me
like an animal out of its burrow and whipped around the tree whistling
under its breath and breaking the air unseasonably with a quick turn of
phrase as quick as the broken wind as it fell from the trees moaning quietly
as if interrupted in its sleep uncomprehending the silence of that insane
evening whenever we spoke it was as if as if went backwards from the
air to the mouth from the ear to the air until that last breathless moment
when at last I fell quiet, swallowing tenaciously

Fake Poem 4

Yesterday I thought that way until I went to bed my regulated waking
thinking interrupted in my dream the shadow of a man walked through
the very transparent window through which I viewed my world disrupted
what I had been pleased to call my chain of thought turned out to be not
a hard discrete chain at all but a smooth continuous though not entirely
seamless skein and thereafter a colourless stream and thereafter again
an interrupted stream broke in splashes on the pavement slipped away
dwindling in a rush of colours never to be redeemed again but never mind
a new skin replaced the old in time and the same two feet stood again too
squarely standing on the ground as always walking up the stairs and down
again and up

Fake Poem 10

You were not born alone,
& you will not die alone.
Someone will be there with you always,
even in that echoing room,
even when you don't prefer it.

Without them you cannot be born, die,
or remain alive even into the next moment.

As soon as you have come to speech,
you can never speak yourself alone,
but always all those others, too,
those long dead ancestors, those ancient mothers,
your nearby contemporaries, those outside,
those inside,
still waiting to be born,
the multitudes of people who have never known you
and whom you've never known.

You are their very own ghost,
their uninvited guest,
their unmentionable sister.

They are your guides. Always present,
never any need to call them.
Without them you will surely become
irretrievably lost.

In the meantime,
try to remember, then try to forget.
The memory will neither fully arrive, nor fully go away.

Soon enough you will go missing forever.
There are so many who will never guess
where you have ever gone.

Fake Poem 11

The way that consciousness and speech are prone to drift when prone and
lying lifelike laying down the letter of the law where speech is strict and
ordered no thread lost or stray we go away from ourselves lose ourselves
in mental play the play of words light on leaves an inner moving picture
a dream one image to the next bubbles and waves arising shadows and
reflections hidden in the stream the odd bright fish flickers in the shallows
shows its colours

Fake Poem 16

The way
        the mind
moves and works in its own silence,
slipping
        so quietly from one
thought to another,
floating things on water,
no seam between.

Never know it's there
until its reappears,
that not quite fullness of the half idea,
the low tide of the moon and mind
passive receptor to itself.

Absence of action or gesture.
Around a word or an image,
lips form the whisper,
the singular aura of singular feeling

all those secret
cracks & creakings
underneath
underneath.

Fake Poem 21

Under the kitchen table with the flour and the cat dish,
in the kitchen sink with the supper dishes and the bubbles of soap.
Behind half-closed eyelids in the sunlight.
Round About Midnight in the moonlit garden.

Two steps down into the Qu'appelle Valley in April sunshine.
Called by name on the street by an unfamiliar voice on any uncertain grey day,
no-one there but strangers when you turn.
Wherever women are talking and laughing, watching their children at play.

The water that falls from the sky is always a grace.
Equally graceful, evaporation in sunlight.
The fact that the very same water is always falling again somewhere else,
and is taken up again, again condensing and falling, again taken up.
Only to know about this, to be able to think about it: impossible grace.

Surrounded by grace, inescapably, always.
Like the ordinary rain of any
ordinary day.

CLEA ROBERTS ❧

Cold Snap

The simple arguments
of juncos retract
into the forest.

The house settles
in the hungry air,
its short complaints
plucking and clapping
at our sleep.

Frost climbs
the bedroom
windows.

This is the landscape
of our slumber,
the bright boughs
we breathe out
in our dreams.

*

The narrow light
of morning;
the wavering syllables
of the radio
indigenous to the kitchen

where you fry
bacon for our sandwiches,
and the rising bread
smells of yeast
or nostalgia.

Let's be an
old couple
someday—

the visible
and the invisible
economies drifting
between us.

*

Maybe
it's heart
palpitations,

maybe it's
a snowplow
scraping
the chip seal road.

You are
the only audience
to my frailty.

—I want to be
a winter person;

I like the way
it implies
improvement.

*

So cold
it squared
the truck's wheels

and unstitched
the long sleeve
of our schedules,

the sound
of distant highways
folded then placed
on the doorstep.

Tell me
how to breathe
between
what is painful
and what is beautiful,

my lips,
my eyelids
slow with cold.

LISA ROBERTSON ❧

Police

It is the summer the movie stars are dying
Police are coming and going
They have made an announcement
With no result
And what a house sells for somewhere
Quietly becomes true and lyrical
Then the moment passes
Like the subjectivity of doubt
Its weight as a syllable
Opening heavily on slow hinge
To an essentially dark garden
Where you glimpse the breath of what you once said
Receding like a ghost.

You, who is the only imaginable person
Help me be the place where
The bicycle, the dream of wit, the obscenity
on the staircase, the gentle book
As meanwhile a woman is
Vigorously mopping a floor.

I'm still trying to interest you in my memory
And its variants
The shadow of a flag at night
These female figures.

Then becoming calm
Where having been irate
Having spoken loudly to the man
Who had refused
Calmly the employee now sweeping
It is a tableau of considerable force
And I will take some comfort in it
I will lay out the comfort
So as to sleep
The sound of the wind has sweeping in it

And the thought of the movement of planets
Is so effortful
I am nauseous.

Those images that have been made precise
Are pouring grace.
Grace is certainly a part of thinking
When grace first came
It felt obscure.

In the house at night
Sociology is futile
I almost cry
With the inconsequence of it.

JUDITH ROCHE ✍

Fishtown, Lower Skagit

from a long canoe with 18 paddlers
Language burned in us. We were wild with ideas...
–Bob Rose

Water rocks under us.
Water pours over us, from a slate sky.
Water collects in the bottom of the boat,
drips off our hat brims, soaks through clothes.
Purple larkspur shows vivid against rain-blackened
rock faces. Columbine in niches clings in shallow soil,
saxifrage shines white on succulent stems.
A red tail hawk drifts above, looking for dinner.
We rock in the river's current, *"Paddles ready,"*
then *"all paddles ahead,"* and *"Paddles rest,"*
shouted from the back of the boat. A mean
wind arrives from the south. We're pilgrims searching
the ghost of Fishtown hovering in this Skagit
rain, but most shacks have been torn down,
the land logged, leaving bare bones, or nothing but greenery.
The hopeful artists and scholars of the estuary
scattered, mostly still around the valley, still making art,
all in our sixties and seventies now.
Some have passed, a life lived for art—as ephemeral as a dance—
but many leave a trail of poems and paintings behind.
None can leave behind the life lived on the Skagit,
the youthful hope and dedication. The river
moves and changes. Shacks, landmarks and channels gone.
But *Rivers have memories,* says Bob Rose. Restless, they adjust
in their beds. Robert Sund is gone but his tight little cabin
is a refuge from the rain today. We huddle inside
and crowd around the wood stove, drink hot tea and listen
to Tim McNulty read Sund's poems of this place. Water,
water, herons, rain, swallows, mud, and rain again.
Even a former resident of Fishtown can't find
what was there. The river has changed channels
and Fishtown has become a state of mind.

Translation

(an ars poetica?)

In the hour of remembrance
a convention of crows gathers,
rattles and caws in the crow tree—
their newest capital city—
and I caw back—
ululating at the boundaries of species,
trying to tell them my *nom de guerre*
from another kingdom—
to ask them if a truer name
might be hidden
in their wordless flight.

It is possible to love without translation—
can we climb these sounds to soul?
Who can possibly understand
another, no matter how close?
My son signs *eagle* and I think
he means, *witch*, so close
in fluttering hands. A struggle of limitations
of the word to where a map might lie.

Light moves through my body but stops.
I walk a frozen river—it becomes water,
fluid and moving, toward gill slits,
those slats that separate species,
rendering one consciousness from another,
lungs I inherited and a given name,
the voice I came with, imperfect bridge
for crossing linguistic fences.

Does my cat know the name of her kill?
Does the lake the name of her drowned,
and the crows the names of their dead?
Where is the Rosetta Stone
to thread across?

Heaven

When I finally arrive there,
after a brief but mortal illness
I'll ask my mother which several-times

great-grandma, picking spring flowers,
choked a bear with her own fist
shoved down his throat

and could it be true?
And for her recipe for turkey stuffing.
I'll be weeping just to see her again.

I'll tell her what I did
with the rest of my life,
that my later poems didn't have so much

in-your-face sex, so she could have
shown them to her friends
without being embarrassed.

I'll let her know how the seeds of her stories
about Arthur and Guinevere,
Abelard and Heloise,

flamed at the heart of the Troubadour.
And that one of my children grew
up strong, though troubled

by the grief of life, and her very complexity,
and the other grew to become
a rare happy man, through his own complications.

And how bitter it became that I couldn't
ease their passage through the world.
She'll remember that as the bitter way of it,

how salmon and wolves
opened in me and she'll understand
with her own wild heart.

I'll tell her none of my marriages worked out
except for the children,
and that my sisters and I still seek

our misplaced childhood in each other,
in spite of how bossy I could be
as the first child.

I'll tell her that now I understand
what she meant, those many childhood nights
when I couldn't sleep, when she told me

it's all right, you are resting your heart.
I'll want to know if birds live there
and she'll name me their flaming colors.

And, I'm playing the piano again.
Haltingly at first, but I'm getting it back.
That will make her heart happy.

The world, I'll say, is still broken.
Ignorant armies clash by night,
and day, with less reason than the ones you knew.

She'll just nod, as if it's no longer her concern,
and perhaps it isn't. I will tell her
we are orphans in the presence of her absence.

And she'll tell me again
the story of the girl with flowers in her hands,
the Pomegranate seeds, and the Underground.

RENEE RODIN ❧

A Carole Sky

for Carole Chambers (1944–2014)

the night of the day you died
the sky was deep purple
you had arrived

from the moment we met I was taken
by your big beauty and your big kindness
that never changed

the last time I saw you on Hornby
Margaret and Sheila were there too
you fed us cakes you'd baked

though you could eat nothing
cracked us up with your jokes
though you could no longer speak

listened as we read your poems

the night of the day you died
the sky was deep purple
it was a Carole sky

there you were and here you are
with us forever

Subject to Change

from *Subject to Change*

I walk along the beach lost in the propaganda of the picturesque. When I first came to Vancouver I never saw homeless people nor anyone asking for money on the street or visibly helpless. There was only the Umbrella Lady at the corner of Granville and Georgia, her umbrella held high above her in all kinds of weather. Neck craned, face beseeching the sky, it was as if at any minute she might lift off and fly. If she were here today I might join her.

En Route

George Stanley and I are friends
we both live in Kitsilano where we share
the same modes of transportation
the Broadway bus and the Kits library

LINDA RUSSO ✎

in ordinary landscapes

the aesthetics of industrial agribusiness—
seemingly endless available space—

rubber bark mulch and careful border plantings
around the new bungalow-style houses

thrown up next to acres of wheat—thousands
of acres for export to Japan

more to see over the next hill, too—
the next hill so seldom seen

except by coyote, hawk and deer—
at the Rose Creek Preserve

on an untrodden path
through riotous native grasses

I lay my notebook down, lay down
a sensual geography

approaching the edge where
cultivation cuts a clean line—

a doe in the middle distance
placing hooves across the newly shorn field

of perpetual conflict, of values operating
in the landscape—the withdrawal

of slowly recharging water deposits
from an imperiled aquifer—

an 18-hole golf course that fits
a sustainability plan—

the cemetery's westward-facing slope
with its new view of delivery bays and dumpsters—

a renegade squash patch rooting
the edge space of the community garden —

dirty striped t-shirt, empty bottles, an abandoned
ripped backpack in the grassy tamped-down bed

beneath Pacific Willows that edge the river —
the county dump's table for household toxics exchange —

ecology's sociality traced in the
crisscrossing of domestic thresholds —

the current state of development —
making poem-level decisions that constitute

place in the landscape of the poem —
wildly clipped or abandoned

the social clutter abutting yards breed —
a sense of privacy maintained

in shrinking distances —
the pathways of gossip and news

cut so casually across the grass they leave
no mark, essential pre-conditions of being

in the world alongside other animal byways —
ants secretly conveying a path to the house

along the overgrown ivy, worms unfurling
a fertile compost trail, squirrels crisscrossing

branches, wires, the top of the house
again to the other other side noisily

RENÉE SAROJINI SAKLIKAR ❧

Carnarvon Street Lament

Oh I like the fogbound morning
hours when light casts a shadow
on my raggedy sweater and shoes 'cause
I'm now what I always knew I'd be
a raggedy woman just off the streets Oh
I sing in my veins a trapped noise
not let to the air 'cause I'm a raggedy girl
gone home from high towers to the ground
Oh watch me that's where I'll be
learning to spin wool to plant carrots in the dark soil Oh
I pound my feet 'neath the big box towers
driven from road to road I'm the Raggedy One
claiming the moon oh the stars the sun.

Ode for Mr. Stout

I

Your breath
sweet with booze
greets me in puffs of cold air.
A hee-haw voice,
but nothing hick about you,
once you were teacher.
And me, pupil, but
down here on Columbia Street
no longer the Golden Mile
we're just dropouts
people on the sidelines—
me. You, you've got

holes in the heels of your socks.
Up, up your gait—away from me.
The years recede, and you lope past the Sally-Ann, into memory.

I see you reappear as Commander:
in a classroom you paced,
back and forth, melon belly
held high in pants. Your ankles showed. You brayed your facts
through buck white teeth
about the Wars
hee-hawing to your students.
We were dumb, yes, mute, yes,
but not deaf to recitation.
Ils ne passeront pas. Revanche. Revanche!

See. Your voice is with me
and hee-haws onto this page:
Mother, in the mansion on Royal Avenue,
broke our best china over her knee.
This was done in solidarity with our cook,
a Chinaman. It was the Rape of Nanking.

II

This is how things work.
You, at the front of a classroom,
thirty years ago. Time.
You, walking down Columbia Street
five years ago. Time again.
On the bus this morning,
I heard the news.
You gave up drinking, and three years later,
three months ago, died.

Revanche! Revanche!
This is all I have for you.
It will have to do.

Exhibit: after-time accompaniment, morning raga for Paldi

from "in the woods outside Duncan, British Columbia"
children of air india, un/authorized exhibits and interjections.

And there are mountains. And there is water.
And there is that refrain that is for this morning's journey by ferryboat,
       such snippets as will be, will be found
                : saw you whom my soul loves, I say to the watchman
in a Horseshoe Bay coffee shop, the words of—

about the village of Paldi
        outside Duncan
            : saw you whom my soul loves,
           there are the mountains,
and water and words,
there are no expectations of meeting. Meet, the ferry.
Horseshoe Bay to Nanaimo, up Island, and there is sureness—
        There will be a meeting. There are not facts to suggest it
Sing(h), this journey, Cowichan Valley.
Now, the ferryboat carries this raga. Now it is sailing.

There are the names, bring them. Insert Punjabi.
There are the places, this is the time, and after—
June 23, 1985. Insert all dialects and languages
        spoken and dreamt and worked and ploughed and mined and
        dug and timbered.
There is a body on a ferryboat: Sing (h)!
Queen of Oak Bay to Nanaimo, replication of a journey.
Bomb-maker, poem-maker. Name the name of the man driven to—

Name who boarded a ferryboat! Name the history of the bay,
and its waters cry, come, *tikka, tikka, otototoi,*
saw you him who did the deed?
In his path, this replication. And know his end. And know his end.
It is jail. It is obliteration. It is fragments. His ways and means, a bombing.
This is morning-raga-mountains-water.
This is a sailing to Nanaimo on the Queen of Oak Bay—

KAIA SAND ✒

At Least Five Gallons Per Second

In the time it takes me to say this, at least 40 gallons of oil will have gushed
out of the Deepwater Horizon site. And now 50
And now 60
And now 70

And now 80 gallons of oil
In the time since this poem began, gushing out of the BP Deepwater
Horizon oil drilling site, I count 150 gallons of oil mixing into the Gulf of
Mexico saltwater.
And now 160
And now 170
And now 180
And now 190
And now 200

In the time since this poem began, I count 250 gallons rushing beyond the
failed concrete seal poured by Halliburton

By this time tomorrow, at least 200,000 more gallons of oil will have
leaked into the Gulf of Mexico seawater. This, as I eat my eggs and scan
the newspaper. This, as I go on, burning oil BP drills for me each day,
despite myself. This, as each second, 5 more gallons of oil defy barriers and
become the difficult ecology of now.

Written 9:10–9:30 a.m. on May 4, 2010

At Least Twenty Gallons Per Second

In the time it takes me to say this, at least 160 gallons of oil will have
gushed out of the Deepwater Horizon site. And now 200
And now 240
And now 280

And now 320 gallons of oil
In the time since this poem began, gushing out of the BP Deepwater
Horizon oil drilling site, 600 gallons of oil mixing into the Gulf of Mexico
saltwater
And now 640
And now 680
And now 720
And now 760
And now 800 gallons

In the time since this poem began, rushing beyond the failed concrete seal
poured by Halliburton, at least 1000 gallons of oil

By this time tomorrow, at least 1.7 million more gallons of oil will have
leaked into the Gulf of Mexico seawater. This as we gather in a park in a
city near the Pacific, far from Gulf Coast, and near it, too. This, as I go
on, burning oil BP drills for me each day, despite myself, oiled ease. This,
as each second, more than 20 gallons of oil defy barriers and become the
difficult ecology of now

I have 'recorded' and then updated this poem several times since the April 10,
2010, explosion of the Deepwater Horizon oil rig. This iteration is at 10:00 a.m. on
June 3, 2010.

She Had Her Own Reason for Participating

She always gets kidded about being a female mechanic at auto parts shops

She also went to night school

She couldn't imagine sitting behind a desk all day

She described her personal revelation and internal revolution—her struggle to come to grips with God, a male God

She discussed why this project was abandoned after only six months in operation

She can be violent

She advised that after attending two of these meetings, that she discovered it wasn't for her

She decided lesbian rights was a feminist issue

She enjoyed her various writing and editing jobs

She attempted to free David

She feels that revenge toward the establishment is imperative

She had gone to pick up her mail when her husband forced her way into her car

She had her own reason for participating

She has found her niche

She has not seen the man whom she divorced in 1977 since she became entangled in the criminal justice system

She has two children

She ignited a bleacherful of men and women with her message about women, the Mormon Church, and Equal Rights Amendment

She is still learning

She is believed to be a Lesbian

She is drafting legal papers to that end

She is involved with the AIM movement

She is just sorry other women haven't show more interest in automotive work

She is now awaiting sentencing

She is the one you consider the real revolutionary right?

She is a lively little cookie alright?

She is under the thumb now of Old Bonnie Colton

She knows of no New York political figures to whom she would have been writing at the age of 17

She talked back

She moved where her husband's jobs took them and did most of the housework

She now had her journey-man's card

She nurtures her children by trying to save the world from nuclear extinction

She needs a support group to develop her ideas

She was beaten regularly for at least four years

She pleaded guilty to the charge strictly on the advice of her court-appointed attorney

She provided copies of the files to a reporter

She received terrorizing telephone calls and saw his truck drive by several times

She shot and killed him

She regarded these days as something of a radical in NOW

She said she couldn't see why an amendment with such a beautiful name and simplicity could be so strongly opposed by her church

She said she did not agree to hire them

She said she had a one-hour meeting with the president and "he's frankly deluded"

She said she supported WARN because it will be an important instrument in the survival struggle of Indian children and the Indian people

She said the demonstrations will be significant as an international show of 'solidarity' among women

She says, I think I was socialized into a more traditional job

She suffered a concussion

She thought it was just a friendly visit

She thought she had something better

She took her children to live with relatives in another state

She used to be married and a dutiful housewife—twice

She used to be resorts editor for Golf Digest magazine

She was a co-founder of Portland Women Strike for Peace

She was active in the state Democratic Party

She was also a member of the Revolutionary Union

She was always hunched over the machine

She was arrested last January as a result of a situation of fear, panic, and confusion which occurred when four FBI agents entered her parents' Albina home

She was denied a polygraph test

She was disappointed in the fact that she helped them form their structure, and then they wouldn't allow her to become a member

She became shop chairman of her union

She was editor of "The Pregnant Teenager" and author of "The Young Woman's Guide to Liberation" and "Sexual Justice"

She was pregnant at the time

She was one of 13 women who fasted 37 days in behalf of the ERA in Springfield, Ill.

She was feeling so damned tired

She was president of NOW, the National Organization for Women

She was repeatedly the victim of wife abuse and shot her husband when she was about to kill her 17-year-old daughter

She was subsequently released on bail, pending her charges, in Portland

She went around asking questions

She worked as a writer

She works as a bartender

She would never be convinced

She's had a few humorous incidents

she's only as rich as the poorest of the poor

she's studying art history, painting, self defense and Aikido

---

I have selected and presented verbatim sentences from archival surveillance files the Portland Police kept on activist and civic groups in the late 1960s, the 1970s, and into the early 1980s, now housed at the City of Portland Archives and Records Center. The language from this poem comes from the files on the Alliance for Social Change, the American Indian Movement, the Coalition Against Domestic Violence, Friends of the Sisters of the Streets, George Jackson Brigade, Mom's Garage, NOW, Patriot Party, Rape Relief Hotline, Trojan (general file on activism), Tudeh Party, Women's International League for Peace & Freedom, WAND, Women of All Red Nations, Women Strike for Peace, Women's Night Watch, and Women's Rights Coalition.

LEONARD SCHWARTZ

If

0

If we are "signs without interpretation"
In place of a prison I transplant a trillium.

If we are signs without interpretation
"I" is something extra to the flower.

As we are signs
Without interpretation

The local line that is the moon
And the express line that is the sun/

Since we are signs without interpretation
This or that   comes to a grinding halt

One can fill in the blank oneself
A logging truck a train a stick of lipstick

The name wouldn't matter
If this wasn't the realm of risk.

Is this an ocean or individual waves
Always the same like on the first occasion

Or ever the first occasion (as Stein insists)
Insisting repetition does not exist.

The mountain thinks in us
We know that much for sure

As forest forms
In all their rain and animal pheromones

Press upon the window
The shade of the tree

And the shadow of one's body
And the shades of those gone

Making of us melting glacier
And solid rock.

If Mount Everything is mostly invisible
And then Toweringly There

If our every triumph
Turns out to be a darkest hour

If the tiniest nodule of sense
Portends either apocalypse or joy

Mountain
Or mouth

Depending on how
Sense is voiced...

1

Down the road
They live in a Buick Century.

Across the street they live
In an Impala with a view.

We live
In our own Century.

It should be easier to accept
Having a home

Neither urban, suburban or rural
"Everything fifteen minutes apart by car"

With its cognitive rites, signs and cemetery,
Grand catch-and-release of identity

As each being passes into the other
In the hermitage of hypotheses

Certain images disclosing
The dyslexias of grace

So many eons spent hunting in the forest
Flipped to the forefront of consciousness

News about who's way down there in the
Cave's zip codes or out on the ocean

Sucking a philosophy that depends upon
The appearance of seabirds

Of which we moderns are still
The sounding boards.

Tricycles, it turns out,
Were just a phase

The *bio* in *biography* writing out
This other, much longer genesis

Just as the latest wireless communication
Provokes a smile befitting Hermes

Which a wilderness of holding patterns at the airport
Cannot erase, sudden dyslexia, grace.

If too often things reveal their own formulae
Earlier than they should and are reduced to genres

It is not yet known which god idiosyncrasy serves
But surely we prize these wiggles and wanderings

And credit must go somewhere, to
Someone, for our particular accretions.

Now I think it is my turn to miss the point
Yet a voice has many arms and builds us a life

Even after language is pillaged of its magic
And flowers no longer know our individual names

Foothills continue to give meter to the way we speak
And glaciers give it weight, thrown boulders

Suggestive of the force of things, so violent
So fragile and so forlorn that by comparison

You can fit any one of our endeavors
Into a little pocket on an ice cube tray.

Does a text ask you to identify with it
Or to imagine that other on its ground?

Maybe my kid will explain it to me later thanks to
The clarity of speech with which she is blessed.

Sometimes I drive her someplace in perfect silence
Postponing our discussion on the theory of reading

Uncontainable wavelet
Uncontainable wavelet

O those statues of Hindu goddesses with many, many arms
Are no false infinite, in fact one could be the reader

Holding her many books, one in each hand,
Passing each suggestively before her eyes

Taking in its suggestion without needing to put
A single of her other books down.

The dance of the reader spawns
More dancing arms with more

Charming books
And miniature galaxies

New grasses flaming near the summit
Undulations embedded in a rock

Rugs of moss, thorns, berries, tender
Thefts, forest vortex, febrile mind.

Here is the tree that must be center-post of the world.
This is the tree that is the center-post of the world.

No, this is the tree that is the center-post of the world.
This is the tree that is the center-post of the world.

This: the tree that is the center-post of the world,
This is the tree that is the center-post of the world.

PRAGEETA SHARMA ✏

It Used to Be that Poems Were Easy for Me

They had my voice and my echo.
One day they became difficult, sordid, elusive.
They stopped containing the views I set out for them
and became dry, calcified, and concrete. Thoughts
were fossilized phantoms that someone else had.
Ghosts behind old birches and maples,
not the former, towering redwoods clear
in shape and magnitude.
Had I become the poet whose writing
about insular emotions lauded her
no future of moon-fueled feelings?
This won't happen to me, and so I thought
more about my future present tense:
I will have written the most superlative echoes:
the ones that hoot like owls into knots
and hunt down anything that turned
my most sentient self into a fallen-down figure,
the one, only yesterday, you crossed the street to avoid.

She Did Not Want to Embody Cheap Signaling

(after *Undergloom* & Nassim Nicholas Taleb)

1.

In poems from her book she did not want to import a code of signals
that took her father's voice
solely for her imperatives
in which they appeared as grenades, taglines,
or hashtags.

And however she declares Missoula as a Western town,
a city in which she struggles to belong—
its wilderness of towering:
the sighted and yet spindly pines, with their melancholia points
of dry brush, and iron-designed trunks
alongside ruined bridges
drowned in solid ice.
She realized she was losing people
who quietly judged—or not so quietly—
and who believe too solidly in their
false benevolence,
            candy nurses and their do-good harm.
                Yet she learned how to deliberate under a sky big enough.

2.
            Now her family is far from distress, in a saddle
of their own inheritance:
immersion into a wholesome exultation—
everything light and interconnected.

What made her father's otherness a painful recognition
also made him a star witness to the truth
of his own becoming, to his faithful and long-buried
Hindu self—a now emotive force,
far from untoward epistemic arrogance
hidden in the language of authorial tumult.

She moved from the confession to narration in order to
construct an affect of irregularity so she could reckon
with the affable truth of black swans and feelings
of too many white ones, and the torpor resting in their probability.

JEREMY SPRINGSTEED ☙

Untitled

The coffee has gone cold
and there are socks to sew

But we were talking about beach fires
and the heat required to ignite salt watered logs

or we were talking about the new year
people keep saying now is the distant future

this is unplanned time and we're wandering around the dark
like my wood hungry hands on the night shore

Seems though that the buses keep running
and rocks on the Northern California coast still receive waves

We were talking about socks and the future
and I was thinking that it could be a time to mention my feet

and talk about boots buried in flames that lick high as my eyes
or the Chinese restaurant on the 101 north

right before the road pushes from the Washington shore
The waitress is nice but sad

I sit with my sweet and sour pork and wonder about her life
and was there a better time in this town

There is no way to tell the truth about it
I'm sure that she's as alone as me but in the situation I can only order more tea

The coffee's gone cold and I've washed the stiff out of my socks
You never see the socks on the feet of the drivers going the other way

But we were talking about the future of small coastal towns
I don't know how those people live but I feel unskilled around them

When the low tide pulls beyond the shelf
I know better than to walk down to the surf

Days before the future happened
an eight-year-old girl on the beach asked me to defy death with her

I wanted to tell her about riptide and sneaker waves
failed marriages and dreams of waves in Kansas
How the effects of the Pacific last

But there has been no moon in months
and the dark skies gather over me and I'm sure they're smirking

Or we were talking about how arbitrary the calendar
and the terrible tick at the end of the clock

But there are trees on those roads older than god
and there are children on beaches bigger than death

there are men who live walking the highway
and I'm not sure anyone misses them

Of course it's romantic to wander off
to sleep in the always wet woods

We were talking about driftwood and where did it come from
I imagine half of the tree I burnt still in the soil in Asia

The half I lit floating for years across huge open space
deposited here for my transformative plots of fire

You asked me about currents
and I was unsure if I should talk about hitchhikers

the walk away has been a steady undertow
still I keep my vessel headed home

I was explaining what it is to be missed
in not being there we are vaporous angels

When I was younger I disappeared
the only clue was an empty room

A girl fell in love with the vanished me
and when I returned we nearly killed each other

now we are both ghosts
and love that we only speak to the memory of us

But we were talking about absence for the holidays
and whether return is really possible

When I almost died in the riptide
I left for the underwater kingdom

the sea and the shore fought over my body
spit up on the sand the cross the first thing I see
rebaptized in the crushing surf
my aquatic ghost watched my landlocked body in horror

But we were talking about holiday meals
and what one can find to eat on the side of the road

and what does hunger mean
Have you ever had hobo soup

Every gas station from Westport Washington to San Francisco
has my hungry ghost filling spectral pockets with ketchup packets

I was telling you that I leave a wake of phantoms everywhere I go
some head north others south

they are more perfect than I'll ever be
they are my Christ shadows trying to get service at a roadside bar

But we were talking and talking
and the ghosts of trees were floating
my ocean ghost was singing
and my hands go on time telling

Untitled

Storing the bones of dead birds that I pull from my ten-mile day
In my secret refuge I've been learning to reanimate
I build the frame using my hair from the drain
November fallen mushrooms for the breast
I've been practicing restraint
I won't tell you what the feathers are made from

I've been plotting shrines for the dictator in my chest
The steering committee in my mouth is doing all it can to keep hidden

I had been sleeping in a bed that knew no fear
Recently I've been drunk on terror again
Waking up dead in the middle of the night
My knees locked and eyes sparrowing

We've been resurrecting bird bodies
on the shore of the lake in my throat
It is a good hiding spot
They flit their wings past the stone of Adam
A monument to what they are hidden from
Intoxicated on hope which burns like fear

I've been holding this country together with my skin
Denied all visas
But I've noticed a weakening in the borders
There is uncertainty in the city of my ribs
Rumors spread through my teeth
I can't even keep track of my fingers.

MARILYN STABLEIN ✒

Above, Below Ground

At Findhorn, utopian community
on the North Sea, people craft homes
from old whiskey stills. On hot days
curved womb-like walls emit faint
traces of oak-aged single malt.
Grasses sprout above sod roofs.

Wizened gardeners coax their crops,
whisper praises, gratitude.
Rutabagas, carrots sown and reaped
by a lunar watch. Abundant supplies
for sale in the shop: whole grains,
tonics, supplements, honey,

bins of loose leaf organic teas.
One afternoon in a village pub
ruby sun-flamed orbs pirouette
above glowing embers yet no visible
log burns. "Peat," the waitress
says, "burns longer than wood."

Underground primordial
organic peat, moldering
swamp dung harvested
from a local bog
smolders like grief
for days, months, centuries.

What Water Carries

Off shore rowboat bucks
wind-whitened caps, roiling
lightning charged waves.
Lines of fishing boats
trawl the wide river.
The poetics of motion
across vast space.

Memory veers
like a tidal river
doubles back, whirls
eddy-like in reverse.
No straight path between
points, thoughts, and
the litany of associations.

In Kashmir downstream
from Shiva's swollen full moon
frozen phallus in cloistered
Amarnath cave, chilled
glacial ice melt numbed
my fingers busy scouring
charred rice pot
with a palm full of ash.

When walking high
desert sandbanks
through sparse salt cedar
forest sandals rub
naked soles raw
like sandpaper.
Soothing then to
wade warm waters,
dislodge gritty sand.

Across millennia
draining, snaking rivers
whittle deep gorges
in granite cliffs. Abrasive,
gritty clogged water grinds
steep canyons through solid rock.

Three Prose Poems
from "Deceptions in Gray"

What defines rain but the transmutation of cloud into falling particles? The descent is not uniform or symmetrical but heavy and consistent, a dramatic down drift if only for an instant.

Rain is not limited to water and ice: there is the rain of rice after a wedding, the rain of confetti at New Year. Coins, gravel, chicken feed, light in a comet's tail or shooting star, sand, salt, dirt or abusive words—these are all possibilities.

A scattered gathering, airborne and erratic, ultimately succumbs to the invisible force of descent. Rain is a release.

Wind from the west clatters rain on my front windows. At night beads gather on the glass, catching the street light with little convex mirrors. Drops, a flickering in each, run, fall, and collide on the outer slopes of the pane.

The force of the wind splatters a raindrop, when it hits the glass, into many smaller drops. But water, once situated on a surface, becomes more congenial, commingling rather than colliding. Like mercury, water gathers into itself, seamless and burgeoning until the mass is too heavy to resist gravity. Runways streak the black night, lined with glitter. One bulbous mass after another tracks the night's weather.

Some mornings an inner rain patterns my window. Streaks are stalks of marsh grass, erect, linear, and I'm in an aquarium looking out. Vertical slashes confirm where waters, in their gregarious joinings, trace the shortest route down. Vaguely parallel bars edge a pathway through a uniform condensation, illuminating strips of an outer world.

Winters are mild by the sound, but one year a pocket of air sandwiched between the glass and frozen outdoors on one side, and the lowered shade on the other side, combined with moisture gathered during the night, created such lush conditions that giant fern fronds sprouted overnight, wild and primeval, frozen in ice.

GEORGE STANLEY ❧

Waiting for a Moment

Waiting for a moment—
the seniors in their apartments—
at this hour—late afternoon—
the horizon of meaning
is just inside
the living room window—

They don't know what kind of moment
they're waiting for—or they could go out & make it
for themselves—they could move freely about
in the middle distance—

They have no motives—they remember having a choice
of motives—maybe even acting on
unacknowledged motives—
moving here & there—like a thoughtless baby—

Now they have no motives but are still
waiting for a moment—

they know there will be
the right moment—
the right time—

*

When the first seniors' centres began to appear,
I thought that was such crap.
Looking at the seniors' centre at Aquatic Park, I thought—
my father is an old person, an old man, not a senior,
there is no such thing as a senior,

but now I'm a senior.

I mourn Bruno Klingner—Andy's dad—who died last week at 91.
When Bruno was 70, Andy suggested he might spend some time
at the Happy Gang Centre.
Bruno said, "I don't want to be around a bunch of old people!"

*

Wild birds fly over the Fraser Valley,
some think they bring avian flu.
Thousands of chickens
burned in big incinerators
on the factory farms
or trucked to be burned in Princeton—
not here, not there,
but oh yes, here, there.

Six hundred slot machines will be installed
at the Plaza of Nations

I put the *Westender* in the recycling bag—just like my father—
finish the paper & put it in the stack—keep every flat
space empty—the floor, the coffee table—cleared—
so the revolving light—looking for a moment—
won't hit any obstacle—any undone thing—
but can look straight ahead to love or death.

Crowds

(after Baudelaire, "Foules")

Not everyone can take a bath in a crowd.
Only the one a fairy has breathed on in his cradle
can get a kick out of the crush of human immersion.
Only the one with a knack for cross-dressing
and masquerade; only the one who hated his home.

Multitude, solitude: these are equal, reciprocal terms,
for the fecund poet. Unless he knows how to welcome
invisible guests to his solitary musings
he cannot walk untroubled through the busy streets.

The poet can be at once himself and another.
Like a wandering soul in search of a body
he can enter, at will, any person's emotions.
For him alone every door is open,
and if some seem closed, they aren't worth his time.

Solitary walker, solitary thinker, he gets drunk
on solidarity. The crowd's embrace is for him a joy
denied forever to the egoist in his walking coffin,
the mollusk-man in his giant shell.

The love men speak of is tiny, feeble, stifling,
compared to this indescribable orgy,
this saintly prostitution of the soul
giving herself completely, *poetry and charity,*
to the unexpected happening, the stranger passing by.

Teach the so-called winners of this world
(if only to bring their stupid pride down a notch)
there's a happiness greater than theirs, and sweeter.
The poet must sometimes laugh at the ones who deplore
his patchy career, chaste life.

At the Pub

At the pub I am pretending to drink at the pub, as writing a poem, I am pretending to be writing a poem. This is a valid activity. It is something that before I started thinking so much I thought of as art, or life, or didn't think of at all.

Hard to say what the difference is, between being at the bar, drinking, having a good time without thinking, and going now, having to insert myself into that role, sit on that stool, and think that is a good stool to be sitting on, the act of ordering a beer, a Pale Ale, a good act, & this role to be a good role—but not quite the real thing.

But I guess it wasn't the real thing then either. I guess then I wouldn't have understood the distinction, if it had been put to me. It must be all this thinking, all this knowing. Being at the pub then, writing a poem then, was quite apart from thinking. I didn't think then. I talked a lot, but I didn't think. But now I think this is all made up but it's all there is—save the body.

When I drink at the pub I say to myself, I'm drinking at the pub, & that's a good thing to do. That's the kind of thing a person would do who didn't think so much. It's good to write a poem, too, and if there's a phrase, any two words, a collocation, to consider it, it and its neighbours, the other words & phrases nearby it in the poem, study them, stare at them till they stare back, till you're not there any more & they can move, make the little positional shift something does that's coming to life in a scary world, coming to life to live in that world, maybe to save that world.

The poem I'm pretending to write—is that the poem on the horizon? You'd never know it.

When I drink at the pub I'm pretending to drink at the pub because that's a good thing to do, & when I'm writing a poem I'm pretending to write a poem because those are the conditions of my probation,

but when I ride the bus there's no pretense involved. When I ride the bus I'm just a bus rider.

The Infant

The infant takes a step & smiles, then turns back to look up at her dad, on the sidewalk outside Olympia.

The infant will live, god willing, in the world to come, will live *into* the world, taking a step, smiling, then look back quick for reassurance.

The world will hold itself ready for her step. The different parts of the world—the doors of the world—will open as she approaches.

Now she finds corridors and now ledges of mountainsides by the sea. All the ways the others live, unknown to them they work together to provide an entrance, a way for the infant.

And soon she is living and making her own way. And far away the police are chasing the bad guys who would corrupt her, and the soldiers are fighting other soldiers, to keep the world open, to keep the world wide, so the children can find the spaces opening wide for their ways.

Their ways through into the centre. Insensibly they lose this sense of making their own ways. They become masters of the partitions. Now they are older and they become the world themselves.

I am at the centre now, I am master of the partitions, I am master of the moving walls, I am the moving wall myself, but in it, moving as it moves, signalling as it signals, I still want my way back from that first step. Back to father, back out of the world, but I must be kind, it is not my turn anymore.

The last thing I see, everywhere, the new infants, descending from their parents' arms to the streets, taking their first step, smiling, then turning back. There is no way to turn back. Sometimes you can stop and *look* a long way back, to see the family vanishing.

At the same moment you lower them into their graves, you look back & see them living, departing, backward, and now you are master of the partitions, a voice behind a voice in a moving wall.

The Past

Why could that door not close? Why could that land not disappear?
The world is large, what to do, or maybe not to do, aware, no problem there.
And as if, as so often, in dream, and in moments of dreaming awake,
knowing this, known already, & halfway between thrilled & hopeless,
you would want to leap, you would want to lope,
an easy exchange between this & an easier grip on it,
if only the model didn't intrude, the template, the never forgotten.
Any change is a change to the given, the already,
the model of right which is the most recent model
that you did wrong by striking out from.
You would incur punishment by just a slight deviation, a desire,
desire a pit opening on vertigo,
& your punishment is to return to the model.
Oh why can't that door be closed, & disappear? The past sucks
like gravity, like reverse engineering.

The Vacuum Cleaner

I'd almost finished the vacuuming
when the on-off switch (that had been wonky for months)
finally broke. I couldn't turn the machine off,
it was stuck on on. So I finished vacuuming
& unplugged it. Next week I took it in to the shop.

A beautiful girl
came out from in back.
I handed her the vacuum cleaner
(the power head, that is;
the attachments I'd left at home),
and as she inspected it, we began to talk
in a friendly way—about what
I don't remember, but I recall feeling
that I was not just a customer
to her.

The beauty of girls
and boys
pursues me
wherever I'm going.

Then I had to take my head in—to the clinic.
I sat in the examining room
waiting for the door to open.
Then it did. The young doctor
entered & said, "I'm Jason."

SHARON THESEN

Man with Lawnmower

In pointillist pine-light
along an awkward bank
hauling the lawnmower up with one hand
quick in shadows, a sudden covert effort
like predator with prey, I drive by and wave
as we do in the outlying areas, his salute
a reflex—I didn't mean
to discover him in this act—not him so much
as what the shadows were making
            a moving-picture of.

The Fishing Trip

Speedometer rising on a flat straight stretch of Highway 16,
crowded-together lodgepole piles either side whiz by
the two-tone Olds 98, windy in back.
Dad adjusts the no-draft and Dogfish Woman
adjusts her crown of a shark's grin & fin, tarp
whumping the roof where lay the great blue tent
& hammers and pins to raise it, big top of summer
in whose gloom we blew up air mattresses,
dusty odour of rubber and sharp rings of the brass nipple
by the Kispiox where dogfish swam & prized sockeye
wriggled at the ends of poles and lines,
tourists filling ice chests with silver bodies of fish,
filleting them with sharp tools
at dusk, the frying pan, the sizzle above the blue flame
of the propane element. Fairy blue, uneven blue, hyacinth.

The Resort of Reason

I love that poem of Olson's that begins
"an actual earth of value"
—it strikes the right chord,
each line bang-on, Confucius
at the centre. When E.M. Cioran opened the Encyclopedia
of Spiritual Teachings and
read "nothing is worth our desire"
he closed the book. What more
needs to be said? Obviously I have wasted my life
and I haven't even been to Ireland yet
or received the photos of the family
reunion we missed last summer.
I know I'll get there someday.
But by then we'll have two dogs.

White Hillside

Long light falls across long grasses—
tresses of marmots combed out
like a holdup artist's wild-eyed wig.

In "Hlagwajiina and His Family" Ghandl says
from their burrows the marmots could see shadows
of hands. Deadfalls bore the details of their housepoles.

Or not, naked mounds. Some knobby,
carbuncular, bent sideways like pound cake batter
frozen in mid-whip from when the earth tipped
& twirled & gravity liquefied beneath the winds
let loose. Within human memory, the ur-trauma.

Some say, 800-mph winds.

Rintrah roars and shakes his fiery head.

Best not suspend anyone's head, the story goes,
for a being from the sea could just flip
the town over. Failing that, strike it
with a red stick. The town shuddered & shook.

Designs on the deadfalls were to call the marmots,
but when one marmot went out for a look—as you do
when it comes to design—
he was caught by hunters. The rest of the marmots
watched from inside the corridors of their burrow
among nettle roots, being missing people
who wear copper necklaces.

LARY TIMEWELL ✒

from **molecular hyperbole**

*

Poetry
: ventriloquistic acts of misanthropy
: the mind already in the afterlife
: designated cherubim of the math that imagines
: enabling sight in ultraviolet light
: pastoral enhancements that haunt the water cooler
: insider trading results in massive fail
: See: implied portent; replete with lugubrious strings
: the optimal improbable one
: "chemical junctions of the pleasure circuits"
: the art of reverse engineering the accident
: *épater la bourgeoisie* patter
: up to my elbows in your arms
: the elite of oddities with the baffles of erudition
: chat-room exchange of diminishing returns
: when emulate to mimic turns
: See: strawberries, sea mammals, piles of potlatch blankets
: See: pot luck, poverty, residential schools
: in addition to the bruises there were the new circumstances we created
: autobiography of the imagination, first draft
: what should have been but by having been written down now never can be
: dreaming you are headed for home but actually asleep at the wheel
: the faux punk is the real punk!
: a fire in the rain-trough that rings the house
: slowly deciding two snow angels are more than enough
: gospel distillation of the nothing that happens all the time
: everyone's eye hear me
: you don't have to actually do anything, but always be sure to write it down
: starts with mumbling something to mom, develops its own cryptography
: thinking about the tattoo a long time both before & after
: a death that informs you all pasts become identical & never age
: a loose line, a lost leaf
: oxygen's altitude addendum
: castoff Usui Depato mannequins in the rice fields of Motomiya
: rolling your eyes at death & equally the immortal figures in stone
: latency, a Nanaimo bathtub dreaming summer victory
: the left eye puffy, the right one fully closed

: blossom regalia, out to the warbling radius of morning
: opulence popping
: See: fireworks above, slugs below
: we are given just this fistful of time, this singular caress
: matches the sofa quite nicely
: doubles as decorative, I must say
: stockpile from which to work to make a life
: the feral text in the oinking of the hour
: a love note written upside down (that's the rule)
: an Ipanema of toilsome derivatives
: retrograde expressions still smoking in the shadows
: hybrid music that can now no longer go nameless
: turntablist! online gamer! lift up thine eyes to the mountains!
: the sudden onslaught of a minor-key musk in a mall
: the thumping amusements
: the turned-up leather collar of the lost moment
: a replicated marvel done in slightly more expensive crayons
: a cranky, old-fart Dogen, caught in the realm of condition & desire
: inflected sunset fresco of the imitation guild
: dredging the Elbe for the great lost Kevin Davies prose
: each intimacy abutted, each revelation abridged
: I think I'll be staying on as an ephemeral photon
: a commercial jingle composed on crumhorn
: that's not a house, that's a carpeted pylon
: no clocks work here before midnight, but who's to know
: interminable fumbling for the switch
: counting down the strokes until we can all unmask
: what you thought backwards from what it is also was
: a free hand trailing in the water, in the wind
: the bray of laughter in the face of the officious
: a rat-trap for my Lit 12 text
: the squirting flower on Zonko's lapel that says it all
: doo-wop for billionaire investors
: tracing the evasions, evading the traces
: life according to the Root-o-Reeni Slim & Slam dictionary
: because later never happens that way
: a bun in the oven & a manuscript in every drawer!
: random atrocities overlain with a comforting drone
: kind/ ling
: the lesser know B-sides of Little Nectar & the Nectarines
: a decision overturned, a sentence deferred
: Dante on sabbatical, gone to Hell to see the sights
: something no one in their right mind would hire you to do

: haywire repairs to rogue waves
: See: walking papers, bum's rush, jive talk, street smarts
: left with only wallet snapshots & the promise of an early spring
: trolling the undercurrents of thought for thought for thought
: the flickers under the floorboards
: improvising medieval carols over white noise
: second-rate doves make first-class pigeons
: goes for a walk with dry sneakers, camera & Shasta dog
: is that a statue or a dead mime?
: I'm sometimes worse than saying nothing at all
: from sad to inconsolable & sneezing constantly
: the quantum physics of pornography
: the freedom to forget your table manners when eating arugula
: all that pseudo-comical 'oh, what to write' in a café in olde Amsterdam
: handsome, sure of himself, but speaks not a word of English
: book comes to final resting place, a stone's throw from 13 Rue Git le Couer
: language closing in on what it is to become
: wasps of waspy waspish pain
: the scent at the of pavement after the wild talk of rain
: stranger in a strange Land Rover, a tuneless Hummer in the office
: the long-envied breakfast nook of Clancy Guy Patrick Gibson
: the back roads the local people use
: the highly impenetrable personal reference as our universal mutual troth
: an hallucinogenic steamboat traveling up the Danube
: drunk & confused but harmless I assure you quite harmless really
: whirled, the way it turns the word 'world' inside out
: contrapuntal catnaps {*Satie no renshuu, aitta-mama no mado*}
: cross the street remember something cross back again
: word asceticism moonlighting as civil service (sir)
: recovering lost time in incremental denominations
: pop-up window on the harbored sentiments
: word, obviously a trick of some kind
: the present is invisible, the crabgrass an afterthought, an appliqué
: perfect control emerging from what were, admittedly, initial misgivings
: a miracle antibiotic, but good for only a single generation
: duct-taped over mailbox flap *volupté*
: Utopia, the beta-version
: a precarious double-life, weighed down with the tedium of intentions
: an indication as to where you might also look, when finally ready
: telescopic *maledicta*, holding the last note seemingly forever
: vacillations of the (putative) ego
: a star over an unmarked, an unoccupied, grave
: new age empowerment spiel of the anatomical mud

: weighed in the organs & inventories of vigour
: resemblance, not in the mirror, but "in" the "mirror"
: on the cell & walking the dog
: defects that glow in the dark
: this 'loves you more than what matters' will kill you
: half-hearted garden of transplanted improbability
: is all you are & ever were
: the earliest, most earnest, grimaces of prognostication
: tedious companion at the acme of self-importance
: outwitting *la nausée*
: KP duty of Promethean proportions
: the marvelous replica treading air
: the human future of the insects at their mantras
: messages conveyed by coureurs de bois
: reading the want ads by the light of the bare bulb at the top of the stairs
: a ritual repeated in changing circumstances itself changes
: winking parabola of the long pier in the setting sun
: debris, intact

*

Please don't send me any more 'awareness of passing time' notes from the shadowland.

I'll take my suffering along with my free milk & cookies.

I'll lie down & touch the baby toes of the bad thing.

I'm locking the windows & pushing the hope chest up against the door.

I'm waiting for the movers & shakers to, like, shake & move on already.

All my friends have words & all their words are interesting enough to me, but.

They are like old guard communists consigned to cleaning the streets, but unstripped of dignity.

If you have the beat, you are free of the need for any faux-formality called interpretative dance.

The revolution is going to start around dusk & then slowly grind to a full stop.

Then we can emerge, like the last of the better coffee & the bitter wish of the day before.

The band moved on from the old songs, got neckless guitars & bodiless drums.

Got a gig in an imaginary nightclub in an invisible Montparnasse.

Verse verse chorus verse chorus verse refrain refrain & a long walk home down Rue Pigalle.

This before the advent of that. That, the particular, the specific, the precise: device.

We only discover the floor when it is being renovated out from under us.

The most I can hope for now is to make the windows outwardly bay

To scoop a reading mouthful of literal air & continue the climb.

Leave it to the retirees & upwardly mobile marathoners to summon the requisite adrenaline.

It was called a poor-boy cap & it will be again, if I ever find it.

Down in the cool ivy-overgrown New Brighton Pool underpass with a soft ice cream.

Words aren't a foregone precision, but they will at least try not to lie about all my love in vain.

Still looking for that generalized overstatement that will give you particular goosebumps.

Still tracking the it I thought I'd never get or never actually got or thought I'd gotten over.

Poetry: a reliable eye-witness, but with regrettably theatrical tendencies.

The real tendrils as they poke through the hand-painted floral backdrop.

Sending out office memos in strict-time tanka.

Going on & on about 'you don't know what you missed by' being alive.

I can see now I will have to watch my every word around you.

I sing the how many times this coin has been & still not spent.

Dawn is spreading on the front lawn like smooshed avocado on a Saltine cracker.

Poetry: meet me at the intersection of phone book & Bible.

I wrote to all the animals, knowing full well they would not write back.

I woke up alive again today, & in a highly suggestible state.

I have narrowed the main character down to a young brakeman in Prince Rupert.

I'm counting on the undercurrent of a universal (totally private) joke to pull me through.

These words are more of the intricacies of the universe, & no less important.

To "infallible sequences of cause and effect" I say, "You connect the dots."

This comes as good news for those in terrycloth togas, to court jesters everywhere.

Poetry: rethinking a minor theme as if it were a virtual religion.

Thank you for the circles, the ovals, for the eyes; there remains this need for dignity.

We can't say where the panorama ends, but it begins from where we are standing.

Saying these obvious things in a steady rhythm seems important to me.

Amorphous falsifications straddle the blurred planes of existence.

ANASTACIA TOLBERT ☙

Little Girl

I.
dear anxious little girl,

don't be a cannibal.
eating away at yourself
will only fill your belly's
rainy day as an umbrella
not a sun. do not suck
your own blood
you were not raised
from the dead
do not make your
coffin a home
do not tuck your
heart inside a cigarette
all your ashen love
on the carpet
all your smoke & flame
rubbed in as if
you never inhaled
only puffed. blow
your bubbles
carefully
make the circles perfect
like peace signs
in the snow

II.
dear wounded girl

this is not the finale
                    purgatory
this is not the frame
where you snatch
your pail
& go to the club house
not the part where
you say give me

my free back
this is not genesis
not the part
where god so
loved the world
—either
this is knot
not a dream come true
or happy ending
—either
wound   dead girl
when will you learn
process is not progress
progress is not program
program is not protest
protest is not presentation
presentation is not placebo
placebo is not permanent
permanent is not plastic
plastic is not pewter
pain is not precious
—either

Not a Girl on Fire

you want to say
your pussy is on
fire but you are just
a regular woman
you are not allowed
to want. it.
you are not allowed
a wet dream or even
one deferred unless
a penis wants
to take. it.
don't. want. none.
you are not allowed to
call a person & say
fuck me unless you
say this on the radio
or video awards
or street corner
unless. it's. got. buns.
& you know you are not
a needy sad motherless
poverty stricken girl
whose father was (   )
your pussy is just
on fire & you want to be
fucked properly.
son.

Page Nudity

you open your mouth
to tell the story of your
sons them being black
the police & mourning
you want to tell the
audience this is not fiction
this is not a let me think
of these characters
& place them neatly
on the page this is your
umbilical cord you are
waving. hang it up to
dry in the daylight. waving
to the maggots to feast
on the bones of something
less juicy with more fat
when the mourning comes
ache & bake slip it bread
as an offering for your
first born. slip it wine
as an offering for your
second waving pass over
pass over pass over

San Son

small things like the

difference   an *o*   or an *a* makes

a
blacked man
be blocked
taken
as
token

a
woman's womb
whored
whare'd
snagged
not
snogged

a
goddess
want to
loom her loam
put
down her dawn

FRED WAH ☙

Jumbo Requiem Utanikki

(for Christine)

The long pummeling gravel road leaves Duncan Lake and climbs up Glacier
Creek to the trailheads for Monica Meadows or Jumbo Pass in the Purcell.
Range, Macbeth Icefields over the left shoulder, higher and higher closing
the distance to that jewel of glaciers I admired years ago from the KFP
lumber camp in Marblehead, the Starbird. The trails lead up to an expansive
theatre surrounded by a dozen 10,000 footers and, as a peace eye over the
boat to heaven, stands a singular rock hole in the wall of astonishment, an
outline of sky, pillar, door—

> peaked back so tall
> ravine-like
> raven flies a blue shirt
>
> ribs to cross ribs
> huckleberry stain
> so late in the year
> alpine wants flowers
>
> dry August drone
> of Tiananmen
> huge corner of sky
> blue cloud floats
>
> slow across that plate
> heaven's table
> the uniform of awareness
> empties the magnet
>
> long ago the distances
> true shirt of the north
> through that hole
> mind coloured to the east.

A little north of Jumbo, between the Pass and Monica Meadows a *punctum*
of cloud floats behind the hole and stops me dead in my tracks squinting at,
into, and through that far-off hole in the mountain. Could it be?

Over the wide Purcell wilderness this shark of recognition flashes its
phylogenetic gills as we ramble over the alpine meadow with a turn back
over the shoulder every couple of minutes. How could that be?

> just a reminder
> what starves
> and suction
>
> only the old sky
> all the way through
> the centre of the earth
>
> you see the problem
> is translation
> I'm hungry

We didn't expect to stay in the cabin and, sure enough, it's taken. S'ok! We
put up the roomy 3-man in the meadow below and the deer visit our piss
marks all night long. What could it be, repeating, repeating…?

Mt. Quibble and Mt. Squabble. Hamill's Last Stand becomes Jumbo's.
These are ochre thoughts, maybe. Thinking *mise-en-place*, maybe. "To
divide is light. It is brain fever." The U.C. hole of Tranquility is too far away.
Is that where the sun sets? Where?

> cauldron of jumbled rock
> what should we ask for
> a walkable ridge
>
> is that what you said
> you wanted light
> or a useful word for hunger
>
> maybe a creek to nibble
> they saw Bastille on a map
> name like an arrow
> empty (w)hole
> "linguistic membrane"

medium for sucking

But the hole in the wall is Egyptian. It's on the other side, right into
Karnak. They'll ski in the precinct of Amun-Re, feathers in their toques.

O distance
O quiet
O alone, alone

O

"...Mountain that has come over me in my youth
green grey orange of colored dreams
darkest hours of no distance
Mountain full of creeks ravines of rock and
pasture meadow snow white ridges humps of granite
ice springs trails twigs stumps sticks leaves moss
shit of bear deer balls rabbit shit
shifts and cracks of glaciation mineral
...and cutting of your height the clouds
a jagged blue
your nights your nights alone
your winds your winds your grass

your lying slopes your holes..."
your traps

Mt Crawford Succession

can see and love
roots right

theory of dissent
beckons

summer high
as she wants to be

that grey tree dead
alive the same

every year succeeds
hybridism

a difficult theory
for moss

the ascent perishes
both each other

close to living
yet summit

the smell of form over
hands on bark never

more ancient viz
dead larch

for instance, if
difference

disinterred yet
this dance

up to perfect
changes less

according to
Charles won

THOMAS WALTON ✒

To Invoke a Curse (130)

Sarah Bernhardt
dead now these past hundred plus years
your hat beshrewed with feathers
alive as the white stripe
on a Bernese dog
pale-faced Sarah, powdered Sarah
lips large above a peony corsage
was it you who bent down
to punch Leonard Bernstein in the mug
to pull his ears, now besieged
by darkness and gravity
poor old hamburger-nosed composer
Yogi Berra, John Berryman
Charles "Chuck" Edward Anderson Berry
these are some of the dead
who, along with their greatness,
walked once, step by step
like the rest of us
these endless city blocks
and budding, March, hellebore gardens
Oh Sarah, is it true you were divine
is it true you once
were alive enough to smile?

Sayeth Cassandra (217)

You have to eat shit to truly be alive. The soft fabrics only feel okay, but concrete is a force of coarse wool and lewd. The ornate visorless headpiece, Mary Cassatt, the cashmere goat. Most poets seem or mean well endowed with the gift of prophecy, but are nevertheless fated by utility never to be believed. But what is so unbelievable about the degeneration of body tissue into a soft, cheese-like substance. Who would argue against such wild heels on the walks at night?

We do not grow hard, despite our rigorous machinations, but soft as putty in the belly of the earth.

With Gary Snyder on the Trail (145)

this bear scat on the trail
a big pile full of

    manzanita berries
    salmon bones
    gary snyder

O Gary Snyder
at last devoured by the thing you love
not the bear himself
but the himself of the bear

yellow flowers and black pods
am I confusing you with Robert Haas?
who was it who sang again and again
of those elusive gentians

here one season, gone the next
black snake, mountain flox
carrion—eating
with black plumage, a pale bald head

it's a wise old bird, Gary
who forsakes the living to eat the dead

At Dusk

for Harry Petersen (1926–2014)

The swallows circled high above the field and the swallows circled low in it
The swallows circled high and low or dove or lifted, the swallows lifted
Or the swallows dove, they flew for bugs in figure eights or flew for bugs in
    circles ·
Or dove for bugs the swallows dove, or dove for bugs or lifted
No doves dove only swallows dove over the field of clover
They circled for bugs in figure eights, in spirals circled or lifted
Over the oak they dove or rose above the apple orchard
Into the barn the swallows dove and rose above the tractor
They swallowed and wove the air above the oak and fir and apples
They lolled and dove in waves of flight that undulated deftly
And wove the air above the field for bugs they dove or lifted
For bugs they wove, for bugs they dove in the air above the clover
They swallowed the swallows the bugs they swallowed as they dove and
    rose and circled
In figure eights they rose, swallowing bugs in rows or swarms or flurries
And wove the air above the field deftly quick and skillful
Or fast they rose then fast descended
They swallowed the swallows the bugs they swallowed
Until the dark filled the dusk and all the swallowing ended
When darkness was in duskness all the swallowing ended
When darkness was in was when it was the end
Was when all the swallows ended
All the swallowing swallows then that dove and rose above the oak
Or circled high over the fir or low the orchard
Over the clover field they dove and over the lawn they lifted
All those swallows over the lawn that dove and rose in figure eights
Or climbed or diving descended
Into the barn the swallows dove and out of it ascended
Until the dark filled the dusk and all the swallowing ended
All those swallows over the lawn
That dove and rose had gone
All those swallows over the lawn
They'd gone
All the swallows gone

GILLIAN WIGMORE

article 1: on hope

a line drawing of hope sticks close to the blue, stretches
beyond the edges, but not at first.

at first a line drawing of hope is a splotch
not even of hope but of ink or something lesser—a scribble.

a scribble is all you get to begin with: food, thought, what will
eventually become your signature, and if you give up?

if you give up you never make a mark at all.

I pressed with all my might on the page

on the page and beyond it—I started small: points of will
I willed it darker and further, pressed harder and hoped

and hoped harder than I ever did anything before: lived, cried,
wished, with all my mark, that you hadn't died.

you died and I made a line drawing of hope—it sticks close to the blue
horizon. I'm not a fan of edges, not at first.

kelp, upper levels

brown turban snail
jeweled top snail
secreted in bull kelp fronds
at the top of the dark
at the movement of surface
snails on jellied safety
on dinner
on filtered sunlight

brown turban snail
jeweled top snail
shyshark, gumboot chiton
what noise? what uncertain
certainty: the slick thickness
of ribbons, green and gold
and bending and waving
thick whips of stalk disappearing
downward

brown turban snail
jeweled top
agitated at the edge
of above and below
neighbours with melibe, garibaldi
oh snail, oh shyshark
march of eat and ocean of day
night and day, the wash of sky
through the grass-green sea

brown turban snail
jeweled top snail
cabazon, kelpfish, hush
washed just underwater
ponderous
slow wander on the kelp fronds
rasp the film of diatoms
with your filelike tongue

CARLETTA CARRINGTON WILSON ✒

didn't it rain/reign/rein

rain
crossed, crossed knee-high fern of froth
root-worn trail stood, withstood
tongue of land hush-wind/wind-hush-up/rush over shadowy lift
linger bee-spoke in air
amid light, limb, rise like sky lung-house bone palace
line time in piney mystery

reign
does one un/become language
decode the wrought-out terror of a terrain
owl-eyed try to see through hands wrestling land out of hands
the blood-hued view sepia-toned
stand in ragged prayers
say you are who you know you are
yet unrecognized yet young the day comes
pooling in crosswinds of skin

rein
every word hit ground running
slipped onto leaf dared the where to begin
upon a tongue bending over another tongue
holding is in the pen
pen in peninsula pointing that-a-way, right write-on
hold tight/hold tighter to a moment's magnitude
bequeathed beneath a black vat's reign
if an owl calls do answer *who-who be you*

the rain that came in 3 languages
for this is a story of territory
of our arrival in the land of shoot/seed Lushootseed Salish
of us upon this isthmus in this "forbidden place" of lake & river people
a sunset of settlers in feather-flight light bounded by fissured-bark
ranging root seed-sound ground of Douglas Fir, Western Hemlock,
Madrona stout stands of Sitka Spruce, Bigleaf Maple, Alaska-Cedar
still standing Garry Oak, Dogwood, Western White Birch
haven of heavens of cries
uncountable callings falling in forest reign

near enough to here fluted undergrowth mottled profusion
of twig-forked trails foot/paw & claw tracking caw in canyon
of eagle-eyed glide fern/fish Duwamish sheltering shade
made of limb-snapped-echoing crack
across a pebble-beach-shore spores pour dimmed-down
in breadths of birth-and-death for the carcass of the past lasts
breaks into earthquakes forms seas of volcanic debris
to compose/decompose/recompose the underside of this under/story

acres of ache is what it takes to scratch/dig/burrow maim-to-claim
yes, capture by scent-mark tussle-and-tear cling/hatch/climb
scurry beside go over/in and again re-write that night for the over/story
grows long-toed nodes in fecund abodes tramps in/stamps out
across a root-mat yellow-vat of shine luminiferous in mists
damp exhalations swiftly drift in cloud-cloak verdant verbosities
wide as the fungi-sky grow lowly-low beneath blossom-snow
in spring rain/summer butterfly/winter-thundered clusters cling
entwined by vine to nest where the broken spin of a wind-borne sapling's
inspect of insect comes to reside beside root-knot hastened rot
coming-up-through-and-into overthrow of undergrowth ripe and radiant
with ruin a reach across the dew-down ground's haze of days speaks
hew to hue of survival yes, surviving the blunt...howling hunt...of time

LISSA WOLSAK ☙

from Of Beings Alone, The Eigenface

The throwback
zeroing in to
stellify
a skylike listener the
talcy sundress an
enigmatic radiation of her
figure
indissoluble
candlelight fleshing off
mirage narratives
daybreak oboe

On being beggared,
the zeals
protect the wars,
psycho-spherically
probe the plague-pits
we fugued-out shades
misconceiving an
end either in
merciless intelligence
or remote inhuman
mastery

The standstill ..
and any one's impulse ..
subsuming one
and the same
helio-sheath

Our Cartesian belongings
billowing into space
insensate then
yet no affectation ..
starting with a whisper a
hermeneut, plagued ..
posits meaning in
a primordial treatise on light
on suddenness, pleuri-polar apparency

the proton spills ..
we elsewhere invulnerably
bury our faces in
watermelon
crescents

How like our
neutrinos
to bring us,
bear on being beyond yet
suckled in anathemas
eigen-eyes
incessance itself
until the neuro-
muscular lock the
glow of Time
to burn
epic   also meant
Time-porn

People just stood up
and cried,
phantasms in infinity
head of a knelling one
when we spanned
for nothing at all ..
could yield to us ..
the devoid coil
light fills the tumour
feels the weight in a
robot's arms

What thin partitions ..
one of us assumes a
face appropriate
to material things
to the openly
'imperfect'
things
we remain aloof
and
stray into nihilism

RITA WONG ☙

borrowed waters: the sea around us, the sea within us

the great pacific garbage patch
is not just a mass of floating
plastic junk the size of canada,
jostling about with jellyfish and
starving squids in the ocean. this
dead albatross mirrors us back
to ourselves. it is a manmade
network, toxic magic in the
making, branching into your
bathroom with its plastic shampoo
bottles & toothbrushes, into local
plastic factories, into the fast food
restaurants that sing the convenient
song & inconvenient truth of
disposable forks & Styrofoam
containers, into the plastic beverage
bottles belched out by Nestle,
Coca Cola, Pepsi, visible tip of the
corporate iceberg. it is embedded in
mutual funds & stock investments.
it is soap dish & lawn chair,
eyeglasses & twist ties, hospital food
trays & squeezable honey bottles,
lighters & lipstick tubes, all bobbing
& decomposing in a great big salty
home. it is formidable & humble, far
away & intimate, outside & inside,
all at once.

both the ferned & the furry, the
herbaceous & the human, can call
the ocean our ancestor. our blood
plasma sings the composition of
seawater. roughly half a billion
years ago, ocean reshaped some
of its currents into fungi, flora
& fauna that left their marine
homes & learned to exchange
bodily fluids on land. spreading
like succulents & stinging nettles,
our salty-wet bodies refilled their
fluids through an eating that is also
always drinking. hypersea is a story
of how we rearrange our oceanic
selves on land. we are liquid
matrix, streaming & recombining
through ingesting one another, as
a child swallows a juicy plum, as
a beaver chews on tree, as a hare
inhales a patch of moist, dewy
clover. what do we return to the
ocean that let us loose on land?
we are animals moving extracted
& excreted minerals into the
ocean without plan or precaution,
making dead zones though we are
capable of life.

the wonder of being several

belt a bivocal ditty to honour the micro & the macro
as symbiotic bacteria outnumber our juicy cells ten to one
surrounded & surrounding, we persevere
through this episode called industrialization
among microbiome evolved with skin & lips, maw & gullet
bacteria buddies swim throughout
adapting & absorbing
wiggling & digesting
sugar, protein, fat
the yummy stuff
but furbished with furans
they kick up a fuss
break rank, revoke immunity

broken lines get parsed back into a cycle where
the big eat the small but the small eventually eat the big
humble ends become modest beginnings

thank the great decomposers
quiet multitudes within
as unsettlers excavate like there's no tomorrow
so much short term gold, long term arsenic
short term bitumen, long term cancer
short term packaging, long term polyethylene
for germs to reorganize

a magical dictionary from bitumen to sunlight

cadence
: the sound of one material meeting another, hello!
: heartbeat, disrupted & adapting
: tree percussion, funky fir cavitation

crushed
: pressing so hard as to lose one's own shape
: tiny privatized homes the size of skulls
: or microchips relying on rare earth across continents
: what capitalism has executed upon forests

ancestors
: holding my body up through cellular memory, anonymous
: condensed over eons into mineral wealth
: material in the headlights, reconfigured as a vintage car more
: retro than we know, heavy metals millennia old

carries
: one act of the written word
: a sapling song courtesy of xylem, transpires to proliferate in
: the ether

ceremony
: shaping one's gestures to honour what has not been lost, just buried
: the music that we forget is music

mercurial
: a host of premonitions, close to the source
: the sound of fire in the sky

micro
: a power we don't have words for
: the Burgess shale in your eyelashes

bitumen
: buried ancestors, unearthed & burned to expand the ocean
: pitched sacrifice zone wherever it bubbles up, hellishly
: excavated

sunlight
: in orchestra with monthly pull, nocturnal howl
: beaming in the future, a planetary revolution, a graced turning

unsung service

for Stalew, the Fraser River

perched on a paddlewheeler, typing on my fraught laptop
on the *Samson V*, in the midst of freshet
big puppy-eyed, sleek river otter silently glides
together otter & i witness raw logs floating down the Fraser
accelerated export to empires south & east of us
quickly doubling sales of tree kill, when we, the moose & the murrelets want
the trees here, alive
tree care is self care
"to restore some general interest in the future of the human species as a whole"
ship's whistle blasts, deep and foggy
once manned by Captain Drinkwater, trans Samson calls
shallow, steady & strong, she faces the port where Mazdas and Audis enter
as raw logs exit, the engine of capitalist ideology attacks the river
constant container activity as swallows zip, seagulls dive
ladybug, bee, placid Mandarin ducks, humans promenade
flip through *Meteorology for Seamen* and *The Theory and Practice of*
    Seamanship on the desk
where does the museum exhibit begin & end?
what will future earthlings find in the neoliberal middens left behind?
microbial murmur: tardy but still need to act up
zoanosis prompts
crossing thresholds, game changers on elder river
footsteps above, creosote beside, and interference below
industrial habit morphs fish home into trade zone
underneath the opaque river, life i cannot see
implacable sturgeon carries on
in the river that brought us all here to this city
the river that holds our future in its flows

flush

awaken to the gently unstoppable rush of rain landing on roofs, pavement, trees, porches, cars, balconies, yards, windows, doors, pedestrians, bridges, beaches, mountains, the patter of millions of small drops making contact everywhere, enveloping the city in a sheen of wet life, multiple gifts from the clouds, pooled over centuries and channelled to power us, rain propels our water-based bodies that eat other water-based bodies, mineral vegetable animal. when i turn on the shower, i turn my face and shoulders toward post-chlorinated rain. the tap releases free rain to slake our thirst, transformed through pipes and reservoirs. anonymous agent of all that we, unwitting beneficiaries, do. refusing the inertia of amnesia, i welcome the memory of rain sliding into sink and teacup, throat and bladder, tub and toilet. bountiful abundant carrier of what everyone emits into the clouds, be that exhale or smoke, belch or chemical combustion, flame or fragrance, the rain gives it all back to us in spates, a familiar sound, an increasingly mysterious substance

MAGED ZAHER ✆

Do we always start from a fetish then—as in mathematics—derive love?
Staring at pomegranate seeds for an hour brings lust to the foreground.
Staring at you brings love's prerequisite sadness.
I move my dreadlocks so to see you as if coming from afar.
You think of something to say and I imagine my madness turning into a statue.
Drawing on the history of insanity we part without a kiss.
I sip tea and enter the world from a needle's eye.
Finishing the tea, I skype with a faraway copy of myself to talk about you.

*

To step into the world of rocks: half bitter and half asleep.
Breaking from this diet of oxygen and ink.
The occasional tendency to inhabit spheres.
I'm going nowhere near life, near birth.
Assigned to seat 15A, it is okay to moan before taking off your jacket.
Need to create time to stare at things.

*

Love is polluted by the deaths we impose (as in drone attacks).
Day in day out I hear the voices of arrows.
I prepare canned beans for breakfast and wash my clothes.
I am ready for war.

*

In the different bookstore corners I wasn't really looking for books.
I was searching for a gap in the world.
Mostly caused by humans.
There were people with deformed bodies.
There were people with deformed bodies from bad medications.
I stayed outside in time for the weekly beating.

*

I carry my body over the distance between home and work.
(I couldn't save the streets from myself.)
Then I log into some web site with images to sexualize.
Love is inaccessible here.
We have—instead—a future to build.

*

At least I know now that death will work out.
I will be spending a lot of time talking about beauty.
Cross-legged like a lost statue I will go back to my old habits.
Watching time changes whom we should pick as lovers.
Upstairs is where we will apologize to the living for the bad weather.

*

I need an opportunity to dress-up and go shoot strangers at the borders.
Stapled to all kinds of papers, I lack precision.
We tried to engage as machinist in the revolution, but we missed the exact
    moment of power.
I am talking about the madness of everyday, of how we organize ourselves, and
    how we work as if work matters.
I am addressing the madness of buying horses.
I have nothing to bring to this exchange. The moment I can breathe longer I
    am out of breath.

NOTES AND ACKNOWLEDGEMENTS ❧

Abel, David: The sections of *Sweep* published here include quoted passages (given in italics) from Georges Bataille, Glenn Storhaug, Kimberly Lyons and Robin Blaser, respectfully.

Acker, Maleea: "the inheritors," "shotpouch" and "marina marigo wind" are from *Air-Proof Green* (Pedlar Press, 2013).

Arnott, Joanne: "an impressive array" is from *A Night for the Lady* (Ronsdale Press, 2013), "halfling bear (eclipse)" from *Halfling Spring: an internet romance* (Kegedonce, 2014).

Bolen, Dennis E.: "Everybody" and "Greenchain Canticle" were published in *Black Liquor* (Caitlin Press, 2013).

Bowering, George: these poems will be published in *The World, I Guess* in 2015 by New Star Books.

Borsuk, Amaranth: "Show of Hands" is from *Handiwork* (Slope Editions, 2012). "Shifting Shapes" from *Big Red and Shiny* (June, 2013).

Boykoff, Jules. Sources: Robin Hahnel, *Green Economics: Confronting the Ecological Crisis* (M.E. Sharpe, 2011). Arundhati Roy, *Field Notes on Democracy: Listening to Grasshoppers* (Haymarket Books, 2009).

Braid, Kate: These poems were published in *To this Cedar Fountain,* most recently by Caitlin Press, 2012 and 2015.

Carty, Bill: "Kiko Is Missing" was published in *Poetry Northwest;* "Ocean the Great Conductor" in *Sixth Finch.*

Cohen, Alicia: "Civic life" appeared in *Coherer* (Verge Books, 2015).

Collis, Stephen: "The World is Never Enough" appeared in *Cordite* 48:1; "The Word" and "The Insurgencies" in *N/ALit.*

Culley, Peter: "Cruel Summer" and "A Poem for the Seattle Poets" were published in *Parkway* (New Star, 2013).

Deavel, Christine: "From the Ground Up" was in *Work Together,* published by Cash Machine in 2014.

Sarah de Leeuw: "Copper River" is from the forthcoming *Skeena* (Caitlin Press, 2015).

Dodge, Jim: the poems, revised slightly—some might say substantially—were originally published in an annual series of Winter Solstice broadsides by Jerry Reddan's Tangram Press in Berkeley, CA, and both were subsequently gathered in *Rain on the River: Selected Poems and Short Prose* (Grove/Atlantic Press, 2000).

Elza, Daniela: "the salt of being" was published in a sequence titled "intimacy requires more," which was runner-up for the Magpie Award for Poetry and published in *Pulp Literature*, 2014. "intimate harbours" was commissioned for *Poems for the Writing: Prompts for Poets* by Valerie Fox and Lynn Levin (Texture Press, 2013).

Filteau, Fabienne Calvert: "For Wren, Turning Six Months Old" and "Slim" are from *Second Growth* (Creekstone Press, 2014).

Gadd, Maxine: "The Contralmirante Does Not Answer My Amnesty International Letter," "the cabin on the shore" and "Berkeley, California" were published in *Backup to Babylon* (New Star, 2006).

Goldberg, Kim: "Spawn" was in *Imagination & Place: Weather*, March 2012. "Urban Planning" in *Prism international*, Spring 2007.

Hamill, Sam: "Habitations" is from *Habitation: Collected Poems* (Lost Horse Press, 2014).

Hartigan, Endi Bogue: "Arbitrarily" and "Dreamed Thoreau" appeared in her book *Pool [5 Choruses]* (Omnidawn Publishing, 2014). "It was a church then" was published in *Colorado Review*. "20 s. elegy" was written after news reports of a private plane hitting a coastal vacation house in Gearhart, Oregon, killing five people including three children, and specifically the news that those in the house had 20 s. to react. Each line was written within twenty seconds.

Hurdle, Crystal: "Part iv" was published as a broadside by Rubicon Press in 2008/2009, "#1. vii" in *The Capilano Review*, 2013.

Isaac, Graham: "There's a Limit" appeared in an earlier version on his blog Somewhereincolorado.blogspot.com.

Jennings, Chelsea: "Before the Invention of Perspective in Painting" was published in *Boston Review*, 2010; "Tonight the Trees" in *Madison Review*, 2009.

Kane, Donna: Versions of "Epiphenomenalism" and "Resonant Frequency" have been published in *Unfurled: Collected Poetry from Northern BC Writers* (Caitlin Press, 2010). "Absorption III" was published in *The Fiddlehead*.

" ow " by Kok Kox is from "Howl" by Allen Ginsberg.

Lashley, Robert: "Thirteen Different Ways of Looking at a Motherfucker at the Club" and "The Little White Dude with the DJ Quik Jheri Curl" were published in *The Homeboy Songs* from Small Doggies Press in 2015. Used with permission of the publisher.

Leclerc, Christine: The excerpts are from *Oilywood* (Nomados Editions, 2014).

Marlatt, Daphne: "a mesh of force" is from her book *Liquidities: Vancouver Poems Then and Now* (Talonbooks, 2013).

Marshall J.W. "Not Let across the Hood Canal" is from *Meaning a Cloud*, published by Oberlin College Press, 2008. "A Skagit" was in *Seattle Review*, 2010; "Strolls" and "50th & Sunnyside" appeared in the chapbook *Work Together*, co-written with Christine Deavel (Cash Machine, 2014).

Lai, Larissa: Excerpts from "nascent fashion" are from her book *Automaton Biographies*, Arsenal Pulp Press, 2009.

Leising, Jared: "Keep Portland Weird" appeared in *What to Read in the Rain 2014* (826 Seattle, 2013).

Martien, Jerry: "Now the Ice" appeared in a small letterpress edition from Tangram (Berkeley, 2006) and in the anthology *Currents of the Universal Being* (Lubbock, 2014); "to a northern spotted owl" was published online at https://landlibrary.files.wordpress.com/2010/01/writing-nature-20101.pdf

Barry McKinnon's "Gone South" appeared as a chapbook published by Gorse Press.

Morris, Cath: "Motorless Replicant" was previously published in her chapbook *Venus & Apollo* by Pookah Press.

Nelson, Paul E.: "30. The Day the Weather Decided to Die" was published by *The Capilano Review*, Winter 2014, and is from the unpublished manuscript "Haibun de la Serna." "Juan Vicente de Güemes Padilla Horcasitas y Aguayo, 2nd Count of Revillagigedo" appeared on his blog www.PauleNelson.com.

Pai Shin Yu: "Bell (e)" appeared in the journal *Zen Monster* (2010) and was published in *Adamantine* (White Pine, 2010). "Iron Chink" appeared in the online journal *The Volta* (2012) and was published in *AUX ARCS* in 2013. "self-park" appeared in the journal *Spoon River Poetry Review* (2012) and was also published in *AUX ARCS*.

Jeremy Pataky's "Steeped" is from his book *Overwinter*, published by University of Alaska Press, 2015. Used with permission of the press.

Potts, Charles: "Beginning with a Line by Robert Duncan" and "The Task Master" appeared in *The Source* (Green Panda Press, 2014).

Meredith Quartermain's poems are from *Recipes from the Red Planet*, published by BookThug in 2010.

raphael, dan: "Moments from the History of Rain" was published in *Elohi Gadugi*; "Isthmus" was published in *Calibanonline.*

Roche, Judith: "Fishtown, Lower Skagit" was published in *Windfall: A Journal of Poetry of Place* in 2013; "Translation" and "Heaven" appeared in *All Fire All Water* (Black Heron Press, 2015).

Rodin, Renee: "Untitled" was published in *Subject to Change* (Talon Books, 2010).

Russo, Linda: "In Ordinary Landscapes" was published in her book *Meaning to Go to the Origin in Some Way* (Shearsman Books, 2015).

Saklikar, Renee Sarojini: "Carnarvon Street Lament" first appeared as a Monday's Poem (Leaf Press, 2010). "Ode for Mr. Stout" first appeared in *The Vancouver Review*, 2010. "Exhibit: after-time accompaniment, morning raga for Paldi" was published in her book *children of air india: un/authorized exhibits and interjections* (Nightwood Editions, 2013). Used with the publisher's permission.

Sand, Kaia: Versions of "At Least Five Gallons Per Second" were published online at poMotion poetry and Poets for Living Waters; "She Had Her Own Reason for Participating" was published in *Tripwire* (Fall, 2014).

Leonard Schwartz: "If" was published by Talisman House, 2013.

Sharma, Prageeta: "It Used to Be that Poems Were Easy for Me" was published in *Clockhouse* and "She Did Not Want to Embody Cheap Signaling" in *EDNA–A journal of The Millay Colony for the Arts*.

Stablein, Marilyn: "Three Prose Poems" are excerpted from "Deceptions in Gray," a prose poem sequence published in *Climate of Extremes: Landscape and Imagination* (Black Heron Press, 1995).

George Stanley's poems were published in *Vancouver: A Poem* and *After Desire* (New Star, 2008 and 2013).

Thesen, Sharon: "The Fishing Trip" and "White Hillside" were published in *Oyama Pink Shale* (Anansi, 2011).

Fred Wah's "Mt Crawford Succession" was published in *_decomp_*, 2013.

Walton, Thomas: poems here that are numbered are from a current project he's working on, writing a poem for every page in the American Heritage Dictionary using phrases and words from that page.

Wong, Rita: In "Unsung Service," the quoted line by Jody Berland is from her book *Walkerton: The Memory of Matter* (*Topia 14*, Fall, 2005). .

THE EDITORS ❧

Paul Nelson is a poet, interviewer, essayist. He founded Seattle Poetics LAB and the Cascadia Poetry Festival and wrote *A Time Before Slaughter* (shortlisted for a 2010 Genius Award by *The Stranger*) *Organic Poetry* (essays) and *Organic in Cascadia: A Sequence of Energies* (book-length-essay, Lumme Editions, Brazil, 2013). He's interviewed Allen Ginsberg, Michael McClure, Sam Hamill, José Kozer, Robin Blaser, Nate Mackey, Joanne Kyger, George Bowering, Brenda Hillman and Daphne Marlatt; presented poetry/poetics in London, Brussels, Nanaimo, Qinghai and Beijing, China, has had work translated into Spanish, Chinese and Portuguese and writes an American Sentence every day. Awarded a residency at The Lake, from the Morris Graves Foundation in Loleta, CA, he's published work in *Golden Handcuffs Review, Zen Monster, Hambone* and elsewhere. Winner of the 2014 Robin Blaser Award from *The Capilano Review,* he lives in the Duwamish River watershed in Seattle's diverse 98118 zip code with his youngest daughter Ella Roque. www.PaulENelson.com.

George Stanley was born and raised in San Francisco where, in the late fifties, he became part of the Jack Spicer circle, which included Robert Duncan and Robin Blaser. He moved to Vancouver in the seventies, and then to Terrace, BC, where he taught English for fifteen years at Northwest Community College. In 1991 he returned to Vancouver. His books include *Gentle Northern Summer* (New Star, 1995), *At Andy's* (New Star, 2000), *A Tall, Serious Girl: Selected Poems* 1957–2000 (Qua Books, 2003), *Vancouver: A Poem* (New Star Books, 2008), *After Desire* (New Star Books, 2013) and *North of California St.* (New Star Books, 2014). In 2006, Stanley received the Shelley Memorial Award from the American Poetry Society.

Barry McKinnon was born in 1944 in Calgary, Alberta, where he grew up. In 1965, after two years at Mount Royal College, he went to Sir George Williams University in Montreal and took poetry courses with Irving Layton. He graduated in 1967 with a BA degree. In 1969 he graduated with an MA from the University of British Columbia in Vancouver, and was hired that same year to teach English at the College of New Caledonia in Prince George, where he has lived and worked ever since.

Nadine Antoinette Maestas earned her PhD from the University of Washington, where she wrote a dissertation on Postmodern Anthropoetics. She also holds an MFA from the University of Michigan, where she was awarded the Hopwood Farrar award for playwriting. Her hybrid poem-play "Hellen on Wheels: a Play of Rhyme and Reason" was performed at California College of the Arts. She is the co-author with Karen Weiser of *Beneath the Bright Discus* (Potes & Poets Press, 2000) and has published poems in *Pageboy Magazine, Lyric &, The Germ,* and *Poor Mojo's Almanac(k).*

THE CONTRIBUTORS ❧

David Abel is the proprietor of Passages Bookshop and a sometimes editor, performer, curator, teacher and bibliographer who moved to Portland, Oregon, in 1997, after tenures in New York and Albuquerque. A founding member of the Spare Room reading series (entering its fourteenth year) and an inaugural research fellow of the Center for Art + Environment of the Nevada Museum of Art in Reno, he is the author of more than two dozen books, chapbooks, and artist's publications, most recently *Elysian Ellipses* (Sign of the Mossy Pebble), *Float* (Chax Press), *Tether* (Barebone Books) and *Carrier* (c_L Books). *Un/inhabited,* Abel's second book, is forthcoming from Project Space Press/Talonbooks in Spring 2015.

Jordan Abel is a Nisga'a writer from Vancouver where he is in the process of pursuing a PhD at Simon Fraser University. Abel's work has appeared in numerous chapbooks and periodicals, including *Event, The Capilano Review,* and *Canadian Literature.* Abel's first book, *The Place of Scraps* (Talonbooks), was a finalist for the Gerald Lampert Memorial Award and the winner of the Dorothy Livesay Poetry Prize.

Maleea Acker is a writer, editor and teacher. She is the author of two books of poems, *The Reflecting Pool* and *Air-Proof Green* (Pedlar 2009, 2013), and one of essays, *Gardens Aflame: Garry Oak Meadows of BC's South Coast* (New Star Books, 2012). She has lived and worked, thanks to arts residency fellowships, in Canada, the US, Spain and Mexico. Maleea is currently teaching and completing a PhD in Cultural Geography at the University of Victoria, with a focus on Geopoetics.

Hopeton (Hope) Anderson was born in Kingston, Jamaica, in 1950, spent teenage years in Montreal, where he studied at Dawson College and Sir George Williams University. He published two chapbooks: *Out of the Woods* (Mondiale Press, 1970) and *Backmount* (Mondiale Press, 1972). He moved to British Columbia in 1973 and fostered friendships with David Phillips and Pierre Coupey, which evolved into literary collaborations in North Vancouver, resulting in the publication of *The Body,* an anthology of poetry and prose, co-edited with Phillips and designed by Coupey. In 1981 he moved to Victoria and opened Octopus Island Books; in 1984 organized The Victoria Sunfest, the first of its kind in BC to present music, poetry and the visual arts in combination. In 1987 The Coach House Press published his book *Slips From Grace,* shepherded through the press by bp Nichol. After a twenty-year stay in Florida, he returned to Victoria where he currently resides.

Joanne Arnott is a Canadian Métis/mixed-blood writer and arts activist, originally from Manitoba, at home on the west coast. Her *Wiles of Girlhood* won the Gerald Lampert Award in 1992. Her essays and poetry appear in more than 25 anthologies and in eight books, including *Halfling Spring* (Kegedonce, 2014), *A Night for the Lady* (Ronsdale, 2013), *Mother Time* (Ronsdale, 2007), *Steepy Mountain Love Poetry* (Kegedonce, 2004) and (as editor) *Salish Seas: anthology of text + image* (AWCWC). She volunteers with Aboriginal Writers Collective West Coast and (in the past) The Writers Union and The Writers' Trust; she is a grand multipara, mentor, editor, and blogger.

Greg Bem was born in Maine and educated at Roger Williams University in Rhode Island. A member of the New Philadelphia Poets, he helped organize events with the Poetic Arts Performance Project (PAPP), among other things. He then entered the iSchool at the University of Washington in Seattle. He spent three years in the Emerald City, where he helped start several performance series, one of which, the Breadline, was regularly praised by *The Stranger.* He then moved to Phnom Penh, Cambodia, where he worked for Open Development Cambodia (ODC), the Foreign Correspondents Club, and the Cambodian Library Association by way of Pannasastra University. He also ran writing and poetry workshops, and volunteered extensively with the Nou Hach Literary Association, and every month hosted the Open Stage Poetry open mic at Java Café. His online books include *Nine Nights in Cambodia, MOMENT, Benzoned,* and *Vaster Landscapes: Ratanakiri Poems.*

After a ten-year stint as a public school teacher in New York, **Alex O. Bleecker** boarded a freight train in Bergen County, closed his eyes, and opened them up just in time to tuck and roll into an old growth forest in the Pacific NW. Good thing pine beds make soft surfaces. He is a co-founder of the Breadline literary series, a member of the RE DRUM poetry ensemble, and an English teacher at Mount Rainier High School in Des Moines, WA. Please pronounce the S.

Yvonne Blomer was born in Zimbabwe and came to Canada when she was two years old. Her first collection *a broken mirror, fallen leaf* was shortlisted for the Gerald Lampert Memorial Award. Yvonne has also published two chapbooks, *Landscapes and Home: Ghazals* (Leaf Press, 2011) and *Bicycle Brand Journey* (JackPine Press, 2012). In 2012 *The Book of Places* (Black Moss Press) was released. Yvonne is the co-editor of *Poems from Planet Earth* (Leaf Press, 2013) out of the Planet Earth Poetry reading series, of which she is the Artistic Director. In 2014 her third full collection of poems *As if a Raven* was released with Palimpsest Press. In 2015 Yvonne was named Poet Laureate of Victoria, BC.

In a writing career spanning three decades **Dennis E. Bolen** published five novels and two collections of short fiction. He holds an MFA in creative writing and taught for two years at the University of British Columbia. As an editor for *subTerrain* magazine, part-time editorial writer for *The Vancouver Sun,* freelance literature critic for numerous publications and enthusiastic booster of several poetry reading series, Mr. Bolen's arts advocacy is widely known. His first book of poems, *Black Liquor,* was issued by Caitlin Press in September 2013.

Amaranth Borsuk is the author of *Handiwork* (Slope Editions, 2012), and, with Brad Bouse, *Between Page and Screen* (Siglio Press, 2012). *Abra*, a collaboration with Kate Durbin, forthcoming from 1913 Editions, recently received an NEA-sponsored Expanded Artists' Books grant from the Center for Book and Paper Arts at Columbia College Chicago and was issued in 2014 as an artist's book and iPad app created by Ian Hatcher. *As We Know,* her book-length erasure collaboration with Andy Fitch, is forthcoming from Subito Press. She is an Assistant Professor of Interdisciplinary Arts and Sciences at the University of Washington, Bothell.

George Bowering is a veteran poet and fiction writer, born in the Okanagan Valley and schooled in Cascadia. He had published several historical novels set in BC and Washington and many poems that were formed in what he and his friends called this locus, a word borrowed from Charles Olson. His next book of poetry, *The World, I Guess*, will be published in 2015 by New Star Books, a press started by him and others in 1971.

Jules Boykoff is the author of two poetry collections—*Hegemonic Love Potion* (Factory School, 2009) and *Once Upon A Neoliberal Rocket Badge* (Edge Books, 2006)—and with Kaia Sand he co-authored *Landscapes of Dissent: Guerrilla Poetry & Public Space* (Palm Press, 2008). He's the poetry editor for the journal *Capitalism Nature Socialism*. He teaches politics and writing at Pacific University in Oregon and lives in Portland. More at www.julesboykoff.org.

Kate Braid has written poetry and non-fiction about subjects from Georgia O'Keeffe, Emily Carr and Glenn Gould to mine workers and fishers; and a memoir, *Journeywoman: Swinging a Hammer in a Man's World*, about her fifteen years as a carpenter. She has published five books of poetry, most recently *Turning Left to the Ladies* (Palimpsest Press); and co-edited with Sandy Shreve *In Fine Form: The Canadian Book of Form Poetry* (Caitlin Press). Her poetry has won and been nominated for a number of awards—local, provincial and national—and her essays and poems are widely anthologized. In 2012 she was recognized as a Remarkable Woman of the Arts in Vancouver, BC, and was writer-in-residence at Mabel Dodge Luhan House in Taos, New Mexico. She lives with her partner in Vancouver, BC. See www.katebraid.com.

Bill Carty lives in Seattle and was a 2013–14 Poetry Fellow at the Fine Arts Work Center in Provincetown, MA. His chapbook *Refugium* was published by Alice Blue Books, and poems have recently appeared or are forthcoming in *Poetry Northwest*, *Pleiades*, the *Volta*, the *Burnside Review*, *Octopus*, *Pinwheel*, *Sixth Finch* and other journals. He is an associate editor at Poetry Northwest and teaches at Richard Hugo House and Edmonds Community College.

Allison Cobb is the author of *Born2* (Chax Press), about her hometown of Los Alamos, New Mexico, and *Green-Wood* (Factory School) about a nineteenth-century cemetery in Brooklyn, NY. The *New York Times* called *Green-Wood* "a gorgeous, subtle, idiosyncratic gem." She was a 2009 New York Foundation for the Arts Fellow and received a 2011 Individual Artist Fellowship award from the Oregon Arts Commission. She works for the **Environmental Defense Fund** and lives in Portland, Oregon.

Alicia Cohen is the author of three collections of poetry: *bEAR* was published by Handwritten Press (2000), *Debts and Obligations* from O Books (2009) was a finalist for the Oregon Book Award, and *Coherer* is forthcoming from Verge Books. She has shown work in the visual and performance arts, including a gallery installation and poem-opera entitled *Northwest Inhabitation Log*. Her poetry has been published in *Ecopoetics*, *Spectaculum*, *The Cultural Society*, and *LVNG*, among others, as well as the anthologies *War and Peace* and *Salt: Poetry on the Oregon Coast*. She earned her Ph.D. in the Poetics Program at SUNY Buffalo and lives in Portland, Oregon.

Jen Coleman is author of the book *Psalms for Dogs and Sorcerers* (Trembling Pillow press, 2013), selected by Dara Wier for the Bob Kaufman book prize. Jen works at Oregon Environmental Council and is a co-curator of the Spare Room reading collective in Portland.

Stephen Collis is a poet and professor of contemporary literature at Simon Fraser University. His many books of poetry include *The Commons* (Talon Books 2008, 2014), *On the Material* (Talon Books 2010—awarded the BC Book Prize for Poetry) and *To the Barricades* (Talon Books 2013). He has also written two books of criticism and a novel: *The Red Album* (BookThug 2013). His collection of essays on the Occupy movement, *Dispatches from the Occupation* (Talon Books, 2012), is a philosophical meditation on activist tactics, social movements and change. In September 2013 Coach House Books published *DECOMP*, a collaborative photo-essay and long poem written with Jordan Scott.

Judith Copithorne was born in Vancouver, BC. Her mother's family was Scottish and came from Edinburgh, where her grandfather was a tailor and grandmother a champion butter maker. Judith received her BA and Teachers Certificate from UBC. She became involved with writing concrete poetry and other interrelated forms. Among her books and pamphlets are *Returning* (Returning Press, 1965), *Release* (Bau-Xi Gallery, 1969), *Rain* (Ganglia Press, 1969), *Runes* (Coach House Press and Intermedia Press), *Miss Tree's Pillow Book* (Intermedia Press and Returning Press, 1971), *Until Now* (HeShe&ItWorks, 1971), *Arrangements* (Intermedia Press, 1973), *A Light Character* (Coach House Books, 1985), *Tern* (Returning Press, 2000) and *Horizon* (Pangan Subway Ritual, 1992). Published work has recently appeared in *fhole, 1 cent, industrial sabotage, West Coast Line, Rock Salt: An Anthology of Contemporary BC Poetry* (Mother Tongue Publishing, 2008), *Force Field: 77 Women Poets of British Columbia* (Mother Tongue Publishing, 2013), *Rampike* and *Making Waves* (Anvil Press, 2010).

Peter Culley's books of poetry include *The Age of Briggs & Stratton* (New Star, 2008) and *Parkway* (New Star, 2013). His essays and reviews have been appearing since 1986. His photographs appeared in a solo show at the Charles H. Scott Gallery in Vancouver in June, 2014, and on his blog "mosses from an old manse."

Born in Indiana in 1958, **Christine Deavel** left the Midwest for Seattle in 1986. She has worked as a bookseller for over 25 years. A graduate of the Iowa Writers' Workshop, she is the author of the chapbook *Box of Little Spruce* and of the full-length collection *Woodnote*, which received the 2012 Washington State Book Award for Poetry.

Author of five books, including the forthcoming *Skeena (2015)* from which the contribution to this anthology is taken, **Sarah de Leeuw** is a two-time recipient of a CBC literary prize for creative non-fiction and the 2013 Dorothy Livesay Award Winner for *Geography of a Lover*. A creative writer, human geographer, and Associate Professor in UNBC's Northern Medical Program, the Faculty of Medicine at UBC, she lives and works in Northern British Columbia where she holds the only Michael Smith Foundation for Health Research (MSFHR) Scholar's Award to undertake research on Health and Creative Arts.

Poet, novelist and raving bioregionalist **Jim Dodge** recently retired as program coordinator of the Writing Practices Program at Humboldt State University. He now spends his time travelling with his wife Victoria between a settlement on Humboldt Bay and a cabin in the wilds of western Sonoma County. His books include *FUP* (a story from Heyday), *Not Fade Away* and *Stone Junction* (novels from Grove/Atlantic) and *Rain On The River* (new and selected poems and short prose from Grove/Atlantic). His essay, "Living by Life," has been featured in numerous bioregional anthologies.

Daniela Elza's work has appeared nationally and internationally in close to a hundred publications. Daniela's poetry collections are *the weight of dew, the book of It* and, most recently, *milk tooth bane bone* (Leaf Press) of which David Abram says: "Out of the ache of the present moment, Daniela Elza has crafted something spare and irresistible, an open armature for wonder." Daniela was the 2014 writer-in-residence at the University of the Fraser Valley.

Fabienne Calvert Filteau grew up in Ontario and graduated from the University of Victoria in 2011. For a decade she worked as a tree planter throughout BC. She has been published in *Paragon* and *Prairie Fire,* among others. She lives on Gitxsan territory in Hazelton, northwest BC. *Second Growth* (Creekstone Press, 2014) is her first book.

Emily Kendal Frey lives in Portland, Oregon. She is the author of several chapbooks and chapbook collaborations, including *Frances, Airport, Baguette* and *The New Planet. The Grief Performance* (Cleveland State University Poetry Center, 2011), her first full-length collection, won the Norma Farber First Book Award from The Poetry Society of America in 2012. Her second collection, *Sorrow Arrow,* is available from Octopus Books.

Maxine Gadd was born in England, Nov. 1940. Missed by a Nazi V-1, later in London. Mom said, "We're going to Canada," which they did in 1946, took the train to Vancouver, BC. Caught a ride to California in 1959, couldn't stay long. Left UBC in 1961 with a baby girl and a BA. Went to see friends in San Francisco. Returned to Canada, lived in Kitsilano when it was a seedy old place with cheap rentals. She was published by bill bissett and friends—little booklets and packets, all handmade with properly aged machines. Her titles include *Westerns* (Air Press, 1967, 1969, 1970, 1975), *Lost Language* (Coach House Press, 1982), *Backup to Babylon* (New Star, 2006) and *Subway Under Byzantium* (New Star, 2008).

Kim Goldberg is the author of six books of poetry and nonfiction. Her *Red Zone* collection of poems about urban homelessness has been taught in university literature courses. Her previous collection *Ride Backwards on Dragon* was a finalist for Canada's Gerald Lampert Award. She is a winner of the Goodwin's Award for Excellence in Alternative Journalism, the Rannu Fund Poetry Prize for Speculative Literature, and other distinctions. Born and raised in Cascadia, Kim holds a degree in biology from University of Oregon and is an avid birdwatcher and nature defender. She lives in Nanaimo, BC. www.PigSquashPress.com.

James Grabill's poems have appeared in numerous periodicals such as *Willow Springs* (US), *Poetry Northwest* (US), *The Oxonian Review* (UK), *Stand* (UK), *Magma* (UK), The *Toronto Quarterly* (CAN), *The Harvard Review* (US), *Terrain* (US), *Seneca Review* (US), *Urthona* (UK), *kayak* (US), *Caliban* (US), *Weber: The Contemporary West* (US), *The Common Review* (US), and *Buddhist Poetry Review* (US). His books include *Poem Rising Out of the Earth* (Lynx House Press, 1994—Oregon Book Award in Poetry 1995) and *An Indigo Scent after the Rain* (2003). In 2014, Wordcraft of Oregon published Book I of his long-term project of environmental prose poems, *Sea-Level Nerve,* with *Book II* scheduled for 2015. He teaches 'systems thinking' relative to sustainability.

Heidi Greco is a writer, editor and instructor who enjoys the Cascadian lifestyle. She and her partner live in a house that might as well be nestled in a forest, it's so surrounded by trees. She's a longtime recycler, composter and forager and can be found picking berries or mushrooms according to the seasons. Her poetry, fiction, essays and reviews have been published in books, anthologies and magazines. New work is forthcoming in autumn of 2015.

Sam Hamill was born in 1943 and has made his home in Cascadia for more than 40 years. Among his many works are *Crossing the Yellow River: Three Hundred Poems from the Chinese; Narrow Road to the Interior and Other Writings of Basho*; literary essays collected in *A Poet's Work* and *Avocations* and the recently published *Habitation: Collected Poems*. He is Founding Editor of Copper Canyon Press, where he served as Editor for 32 years.

Endi Bogue Hartigan's second book of poetry *Pool [5 choruses]* was selected for the Omnidawn Open Prize and released from Omnidawn publishing in April, 2014. Her first book *One Sun Storm*, published by the Center for Literary Publishing at Colorado State University in 2008, was selected for the Colorado Prize for Poetry and was a finalist for the Oregon Book Award. Her work has appeared in magazines and anthologies including *New American Writing, Verse, Chicago Review, Colorado Review, VOLT, Free Verse, Peep/Show, Tinfish, Salt, Jack London is Dead*, as well as a collaborative chapbook, *out of the flowering ribs*, created with visual artist Linda Hutchins. In recent years she created collaborative works as a member of 13 Hats, an artist writer collective. She works in higher education and lives in Portland, Oregon, with her husband and son.

jared hayes tends to shadows and their ghosts in Portland, Oregon. hayes is the author of *The Dead Love* (Black Radish Books, 2012) and *Bandit* (Little Red Leaves' Textile Series, 2012). enjoys being in the company of the Dusie Kollektiv, Black Radish Books and Livestock Editions. jared's poetry can be found.

Crystal Hurdle teaches English and Creative Writing at Capilano University in North Vancouver. In October 2007 she was Guest Poet at the International Sylvia Plath Symposium at the University of Oxford, reading from *After Ted & Sylvia: Poems* (Ronsdale Press, 2003). Her poetry and prose have been published in many journals, including *Canadian Literature, The Literary Review of Canada, Event, Bogg, Fireweed* and *The Dalhousie Review*. Crystal was Fiction Editor of *The Capilano Review* in the late eighties and sat on its board of directors for several years. *Teacher's Pets*, a teen novel in verse, has just been published by Tightrope Books, and she's pleased to be working on another.

Graham Isaac is a writer, illustrator, organizer and performer who grew up in and around Seattle. He has co-run several regional reading series, including Claustrophobia, the Five Alarms Greenwood Lit Crawl, DaDaeDal, Basement Poetry, as well as co-founding The Crunch, one of South Wales' premiere open mics. He holds a Masters of Creative and Media Writing from the University of Wales Swansea and his work has appeared in *Hoarse, Jeopardy, As Much As We Put In: A Poetry Night Anthology, Licton Springs Review* and more. He lives in Seattle and is allergic to cats.

Chelsea Jennings lives in Seattle and teaches at the University of Washington Bothell. She is the recipient of a "Discovery"/*Boston Review* award, and her poetry has appeared in such places as the *Madison Review, Black Warrior Review, Mississippi Review* and *Sugar House Review*.

Donna Kane lives in Rolla, BC. The author of two books of poetry, her poems, short stories, essays and reviews have appeared in journals and magazines across Canada as well as in several anthologies, most recently *I Found it at the Movies: An Anthology of Film Poems* (Guernica Press, 2014) and *Best Canadian Poetry 2013* (Tightrope Books). For years Kane has been organizing literary readings, art festivals, writer-in-residence programs, and artist retreats throughout the Peace-Liard region. In 2014 she completed an MFA at UBC, for which she received an SSHRC Joseph Bombardier Canada Graduate Scholarship. Kane works as executive director of the Northern Lights College Foundation in Dawson Creek and as executive director of the Peace Liard Regional Arts Council.

Joseph F. Keppler is a steel sculptor and arts writer who lives in West Seattle. His home and garden are an art gallery in process. His welding studio is in Ballard. He believes philosophy and critical thinking are crucial for contemporary artists developing our future art history. His work recognizes visual and verbal arts' importance as culture and that culture is what is least understood and most devitalized by power and its distributive bureaucracies. The artist's patient mind is what lasts in art. Keppler is contributing editor for *E·ratio*, an internet arts journal from New York City: http://eratiopostmodernpoetry.com/editor_Keppler.html.

Kok Kox is Cascadia born and raised, named there by their parents, named anew there in 2014 by themself. Kox has published poetry widely under their given name for many years, but now wants their poems, not their identity, to be their audience's sole focus.

Larissa Lai is the author of two novels, *When Fox Is a Thousand* and *Salt Fish Girl;* two books of poetry, *sybil unrest* (with Rita Wong) and *Automaton Biographies;* a chapbook, *Eggs in the Basement;* and most recently, a critical book, *Slanting I, Imagining We: Asian Canadian Literary Production in the 1980s and 1990s.* A recipient of the Astraea Foundation Emerging Writers' Award, she has been shortlisted for the *Books in Canada* First Novel Award, the Tiptree Award, the Sunburst Award, the City of Calgary W.O. Mitchell Award, the bpNichol Chapbook Award and the Dorothy Livesay Prize. A long time denizen of Vancouver, BC, she currently directs The Insurgent Architects' House for Creative Writing at the University of Calgary.

GP Lainsbury was born in the Great Plains, but has lived most of his life either in, or in areas of, the continent's Cordilleran spine east of and adjacent to, Cascadia. He graduated from high school in Kamloops, BC, on the Okanagan-Thompson Plateau, and then moved to Calgary to earn degrees while waiting out the 1980s. His dissertation on Raymond Carver (Simon Fraser University) was published by Routledge in 2004, by which time GP had drifted north to teach at Northern Lights College, located at the farthest northwest extension of the western Canadian sedimentary basin (northernmost extension of the imaginary political entity Texlahoma that is pretty much contiguous with the east slope of the Cordillera from Liard to Mehico). There he, after titanic struggles with a humility bordering on dread, published his long poem *Versions of North* (Caitlin Press) in 2011, and now awaits various extinctions.

A semifinalist for the PEN/Rosenthal fellowship, **Robert Lashley** has had poems published in such Journals as *Feminete, No Regrets* and *Your Hands, Your Mouth*. His work was also featured in *Many Trails to the Summit*, an anthology of Northwest form and lyric poetry. In May of 2014 he won the Cascadia Poetry Festival's beer slam title. His full length book *The Homeboy Songs* was published by Small Doggies press in 2014.

Christine Leclerc lives in Vancouver/Coast Salish Territory.

Jared Leising is the author of a chapbook—*The Widows and Orphans of Winesburg, Ohio*—and a long-time volunteer for 826 Seattle. Before moving to the Northwest he received his MFA in Creative Writing from the University of Houston, and in 2010, Jared curated the Jack Straw Writers Program. Currently, he's teaching English at Cascadia Community College.

Christine Lowther is the author of three poetry collections and co-editor and co-author of two anthologies: *Writing the West Coast: In Love with Place* and *Living Artfully: Reflections from the Far West Coast*. Her work has appeared as Poetry In Transit and in *subTerrain, Poetry is Dead, Lake, Quills, Other Voices, The New Quarterly, The Fiddlehead* and *Room*. Her work is included in *Force Field: 77 Women Poets of British Columbia, In the Company of Animals, Walk Myself Home, Risking for Change, Salt in Our Blood, Crowlogue, Wild Moments: Adventures with Animals in the North* and *Love Where the Nights are Twice as Long*. Christine lives on a floathouse in Clayoquot Sound on Vancouver Island where she enjoys swimming.

Daphne Marlatt, poet, novelist, essayist, oral historian and Noh dramatist, has been writing and publishing for four decades. Her many titles include *Vancouver Poems, Steveston*, and most recently, *Liquidities: Vancouver Poems Then and Now*, as well as the novels *Zócalo, Ana Historic* and *Taken*. Her novelistic long poem *The Given* received the 2009 Dorothy Livesay Award. She was awarded the George Woodcock Lifetime Achievement Award for her work in 2012.

J.W. Marshall was brought to Seattle at age seven in 1959 after his father retired from the military. He holds degrees from Seattle Central Community College, the University of Washington, the University of Iowa and Seattle University, but the best education he has received came and continues to come from co-owning and operating Open Books, a bookstore founded in 1987 which became poetry-only in 1995. The customers and the books are company of the highest order. His first full-length book, *Meaning a Cloud*, won the Field Poetry Prize and was published in 2008 by Oberlin College Press.

Jerry Martien has lived in the Humboldt Bay region since 1970, working as a night watchman, truck driver, bookstore clerk and carpenter for two decades. He has taught in rural classrooms through the California Poets in the Schools program, and as a lecturer at Humboldt State University, where he's presently teaching environmental writing. A political activist, he has organized and served on many boards and committees and lunatic fringe groups. He is the author of *Shell Game: A True Account of Beads and Money in North America,* several chapbooks of poetry, and a collection, *Pieces in Place.*

Susan McCaslin is the author of thirteen volumes of poetry, including *The Disarmed Heart* (The St. Thomas Poetry Series, 2014). Her previous volume *Demeter Goes Skydiving* was shortlisted for the BC Book Prize and the first-place winner of the Alberta Book Publishing Award in 2012. Susan lives in Fort Langley, British Columbia, where she organized the Han Shan Poetry Initiative to help save a rainforest in Langley. www.susanmccaslin.ca.

Frances McCue is a poet, essayist, reviewer and arts instigator. From 1996–2006 she was the founding director of Richard Hugo House in Seattle. Her second poetry collection, *The Bled*, published by Factory Hollow Press, won the Washington State Book Award in 2011. *The Car that Brought You Here Still Runs*, her book of essays about Richard Hugo and the Northwest Towns that he wrote poems about, is named after a line in Hugo's epic poem "Degrees of Gray in Philipsburg." That book was a runner up for the Washington State book award, also in 2011. Her other book of poems is *The Stenographer's Breakfast* and another book of prose, *Mary Randlett Portraits*, is forthcoming in September, 2014. Currently, she is the Writer in Residence in the University of Washington's Undergraduate Honors Program where she is the 2013 "Teacher of Distinction." www.francesmccue.com.

Andy Meyer was born in northern Iowa and attended Luther College in Decorah before moving to Seattle in 2004 to study literature at the University of Washington. He received a PhD in English from the UW in 2010. Having taught numerous courses in both UW's English Department and its Program on the Environment, he now teaches Humanities at The Northwest School. He lives in Seattle's Central District.

Ottawa-born Vancouver resident and member of the TADS poetry group (George Bowering, George Stanley, Jamie Reid, Chris Turnbull, Renee Rodin, Ryan Knighton, Wayde Compton, and Reg Johansson), **Cath Morris** has been writing poetry and stories since she was a child. Besides her chapbook, *Venus & Apollo*, from Pookah Press (2009), Cath's poetry has been published in *TADS, Urban Pie* and *The Capilano Review*, as well as in the online poetry journals *Ottawater.com, Poethia.com* and *Bywords.ca*. Her work also appears in Coach House Press' anthology for Poet Laureate George Bowering's seventieth birthday, *71(+) for GB*, and Corporate Watch UK's 10th Anniversary Anthology in Oxford (2007). In 1998, Irina Trouchenko staged the one-act play, *An Artist's Dream*, based on Cath's and Chris Turnbull's poetry, at UBC's Chan Centre. Cath currently works both as an Academic Editor and as a Researcher for an aboriginal television producer in Vancouver.

By day **Peter Munro** works as a fisheries scientist, on deck in the Bering Sea, the Gulf of Alaska, and the Aleutian Islands, or chained to a computer in Seattle. By night, Munro makes poems. Some have been published or are forthcoming in *Poetry*, the *Beloit Poetry Journal*, the *Iowa Review*, the *Birmingham Poetry Review*, *Passages North*, *The Cortland Review*, *The Valparaiso Poetry Review*, *Compose* and elsewhere. Listen to more poems at www.munropoetry.com, where you will be protected under an iron-clad, money-back guarantee.

Amber Nelson lives, bikes and hikes in Cascadia. She is the co-founder and poetry editor of *alice blue review* and the founding editor of alice blue books and Shotgun Wedding. She is the author of several chapbooks. Her first full-length book, *In Anima: Urgency*, is available from Coconut Books. Her second book, *The Human Seasons*, is forthcoming, also from Coconut.

Doug Nufer writes poetry and prose based on formal constraints. His poetry collections include *Lounge Acts* (Insert Blanc, 2013), *We Were Werewolves* (Make Now, 2008) and *The Dammed* (ubu.com, 2011), which also is the basis for a 2014 installation/performance at the Hedreen Gallery at Seattle U., with a movie by Amy Billharz. His novels include *Negativeland* (Autonomedia, 2004), *Never Again* (Black Square, 2004),

By Kelman Out of Pessoa (Les Figues, 2011) and *Lifeline Rule* (Spuyten Duyvil, 2015). He often performs with musicians, dancers, the word band Interrupture, and/or solo. He lives in Seattle, where he runs a wine shop. These are sections of *The Me Theme,* his book-length poem, in which strings of letters must be repeated to form different lines. Some of this has appeared in *The Monarch Review.*

John Olson currently works as a stripper in a piano bar. He is old enough to remember when the floorboards of hardware stores creaked and heavyset men with walrus mustaches actually knew something about tools. His favorite song is "I am the Walrus" but only if it's played on a hydrogen jukebox at the 18th Street Coffeehouse in Santa Monica. He is the author of eight books of poetry, the most recent of which is *Larynx Galaxy* (Black Widow Press, 2012). He has also authored three novels, including *Souls of Wind, The Nothing That Is,* and *The Seeing Machine. Essences and Sentences,* a collection of essays, is forthcoming from Ravenna Press; another novel, *My Other Car is a Bed in Paris,* is forthcoming from Quale Press. Olson is the three-time recipient of a Fund for Poetry Award and The Stranger's annual genius award for literature in 2004. In 2012 Olson was one of eight finalists for an Artist Trust Arts Innovator Award, and in 2008 *Souls of Wind* was shortlisted for a Believer book of the year award.

Catherine Owen lives in New Westminster, BC. She is the author of ten collections of poetry, among them *Trobairitz* (Anvil Press, 2012), *Seeing Lessons* (Wolsak & Wynn, 2010) and *Frenzy* (Anvil Press, 2009). Her poems are included in several recent anthologies such as *Forcefield: 77 Women Poets of BC* (Mothertongue Press, 2013). Her collection of memoirs and essays is called *Catalysts: confrontations with the muse* (W&W, 2012). *Frenzy* won the Alberta Book Prize, and other collections have been nominated for the BC Book Prize, the ReLit, the CBC Prize and the George Ryga Award. Owen edits, tutors, plays metal bass, works on the TV show, *Arrow,* collaborates on multimedia exhibits and co-runs Above & Beyond chapbook productions. Her book of elegies, *Designated Mourner,* was released by ECW Press in 2014, and a chapbook called *Rivulets* is out from The Alfred Gustav Press. In 2015, Wolsak & Wynn will publish her compendium on the practices of writing called *The Other 23 & a Half Hours: Or Everything You Wanted to Know that Your MFA Didn't Teach You.*

Shin Yu Pai is the author of several poetry collections, including *Aux Arcs* (La Alameda, 2013), *Adamantine* (White Pine, 2010), *Sightings* (1913 Press, 2008) and *Equivalence* (La Alameda, 2003). She has been a writer-in-residence for the Seattle Art Museum and has curated programs for SAM WORD and On the Boards. She contributes arts and literary criticism to *Northwest Asian Weekly* and *International Examiner.* Shin Yu received her MFA from The School of the Art Institute of Chicago and studied also at Naropa University, where she received the Hiro Yamagata and Zora Neale Hurston scholarships. Shin Yu is a 2014 Stranger Genius Nominee in Literature and a three-time fellow of the MacDowell Colony. For more information, visit http://shinyupai.com.

Jeremy Pataky grew up in northern Idaho and earned a BA at Western Washington University and an MFA from the University of Montana. His first book of poetry, published in the Alaska Literary Series by University of Alaska Press, is called *Overwinter* (2015). He has thoroughly explored the coast of British Columbia and parts of Southeast Alaska by sailboat. His off-grid cabin in Wrangell-St. Elias National Park is not far from Mount St. Elias and Cascadia's wild, north-most reaches.

The Source from Green Panda Press (2014) is **Charles Potts'** most recent publication. Other books in print are *Valga Krusa* in two volumes, *Yellow Christ* and *Laffing Water* from Green Panda Press; *The Portable Potts* and *Inside Idaho* from West End Press; *Kiot, Lost River Mountain,* and *Slash and Burn* with Robert McNealy from Blue Begonia Press; a reprint of *Little Lord Shiva: The Berkeley Poems, 1968* from Glass Eye Books; *Nature Lovers* from Pleasure Boat Studio; and *Across the North Pacific* from Slough Press in College Station, Texas. Potts published books by thirty other poets and was the editor/publisher of *Litmus* and *The Temple* magazines. *The Malpais Review,* a quarterly from Placitas, New Mexico, recently published his critical work on Charles Olson and Edward Dorn. He has donated his literary archive to the Merrill-Cazier Library at Utah State University in Logan, Utah. Potts has been publishing since 1963.

Seattle Born! **C.E. Putnam** is a text, image and sound artist currently living in Portland, Oregon, where he operates the Putnam Institute for Space Opera Research (P.I.S.O.R.). He has lived in London, Washington, DC, Bangkok and, most recently, Singapore. Author of six books: *The Papier-Mâché Taj Mahal* (1997), *XX Elegies* (1998), *Spaces Where Spaces Are* (1999), *Transmissions from the Institute* (2000), *Maniac Box* (2001), *Things Keep Happening* (2003). He is also the co-author with Daniel Comiskey of a book-length collaboration, *Crawlspace* (2007). He is currently working on a multi-volume work entitled "The Bunny Manuscript."

Meredith Quartermain is a poet and story-writer living in Vancouver, BC. Her first book of poetry, *Vancouver Walking* (NeWest Press), won a BC Book Award; *Recipes from the Red Planet* (BookThug) was a finalist for a BC Book Award; and *Nightmarker* (BookThug) was a finalist for a Vancouver Book Award. *Rupert's Land,* a novel (BookThug), explores aboriginal/settler relations in 30s dustbowl Alberta, and a new collection of stories *I, Bartleby* is forthcoming from Talonbooks in 2015. In 2002, she cofounded Nomados Press, publishers of numerous chapbooks of innovative Canadian and US writing.

dan raphael has been active in Cascadia for over three decades as poet, performer, publisher and reading host. His most recent books are *The State I'm In* (nine muses books) and *Impulse & Warp* (Wordcraft of Oregon). Current poems appear in *Phantom Drift, Caliban, Elohi Gadugi, Giants Among Us* and *Big Bridge.*

In the early 1960s **Jamie Reid** was one of the original five editors of Vancouver's *TISH* magazine, along with other British Columbia poets George Bowering, Frank Davey, David Dawson and Fred Wah. After a sabbatical of nearly twenty years from publishing while militating as a political activist, he produced *Prez: Homage to Lester Young,* in 1994 with Oolichan Books, followed by *I. Another. The Space Between,* from Talonbooks in 2004. During the 1990s, he also published a magazine of poetry and commentary called *DaDaBaBy.* He usually writes about language, consciousness and politics. The music of language is important to him.

Clea Roberts lives on the outskirts of Whitehorse, Yukon. Her debut collection of poems, *Here Is Where We Disembark* (Freehand 2010), was a finalist for the Gerald Lampert Award for best first book of poetry in Canada and was published in German by Edition Rugerup (2013). Clea's poems have been published in journals and anthologies in Canada, the United Kingdom and Australia. She has received fellowships from the Vermont Studio Centre, the Atlantic Centre for the Arts, the Banff Centre for the Arts and is a five-time recipient of the Yukon Government Advanced Artist Award. Clea was the founder and organizer of the Whitehorse Poetry Festival and she currently runs the Kicksled Reading Series.

Lisa Robertson was born in Toronto, but came to Cascadia as soon as she was free to do so, at the age of 17. She lived at Musgrave Landing on Salt Spring Island for several years before moving to Vancouver to study at Simon Fraser University with Roy Miki, Rob Dunham, George Bowering and Robin Blaser in the mid 80s. She was a collective member of KSW for twelve years, and is an honorary board member of Artspeak Gallery. She now lives in the Vienne region of France, and travels frequently to teach and to lecture—Cambridge, Berkeley, Paris, Rotterdam and most recently at Princeton University. New Star continues to reprint her first three books of poetry, *XEclogue*, *Debbie* and *The Weather*. Her collection of essays on urbanism and architecture in Cascadia, *Occasional Works and Seven Walks from the Office for Soft Architecture*, came out in 2003 with Clear Cut, in Astoria, and has been reissued by Coach House Books who have also recently published her new long poem, *Cinema of the Present*.

Judith Roche has won two American Book Awards and published three collections of poetry. A fourth, *All Fire All Water*, will appear early in 2015 from Black Heron Press. She has taught at all levels from elementary to university and in prisons. She has poems installed in several Seattle area public art installations and is widely published in magazines and journals. She is a Fellow in the Black Earth Institute, an organization dedicated to social justice, environmental issues and spiritual awareness.

Renee Rodin was born in Montreal, Quebec, and came to the West Coast in the late sixties. Her books include *Bread and Salt* (Talonbooks), *Ready for Freddy* (Nomados) and *Subject To Change* (Talonbooks). She is currently working on a new manuscript.

Linda Russo is the author of three books of poetry, including *The Enhanced Immediacy of the Everyday* (Chax Press, 2014) and *Meaning to Go to the Origin in Some Way* (Shearsman Books, 2015) and a collection of lyric essays *To Think of Her Writing Awash in Light* (Subito, 2015). She's also published several scholarly essays, most recently in *Among Friends: Engendering the Social Site of Poetry* (University of Iowa Press, 2013). She lives in the Columbia River Watershed (eastern Washington State, US, America). inhabitorypoetics.blogspot.com

Renée Sarojini Saklikar writes *thecanadaproject,* a life-long poem chronicle that includes poetry, fiction, and essays. Published work from the project appears in journals, anthologies and newspapers, including *ti-TCR/a web folio (The Capilano Review)*, *Literary Review of Canada*, *Vancouver Review*, *Geist*, *Poetry is Dead*, *SubTerrain*, *Arc Poetry Magazine* and many more. The first completed book from *thecanadaproject* is *children of air india, un/authorized exhibits and interjections* (Nightwood Editions, 2013), winner of the 2014 Canadian Authors Literary Award for poetry, which recognizes the best full-length English-language book of poems for adults by a Canadian writer. This book of elegies was a finalist for the Dorothy Livesay Poetry Prize. A mentor and instructor for SFU's writing and publishing program, Renée is the co-founder of a new poetry reading series, *Lunch Poems at SFU*.

Kaia Sand is the author of several collections of poetry, including two Tinfish Press collections—the forthcoming *A Tale of Magicians Who Puffed Up Money that Lost Its*

Puff and the walking investigation of Portland, Oregon, *Remember to Wave*. Sand co-authored with Jules Boykoff *Landscapes of Dissent: Guerrilla Poetry and Public Space*. With Garrick Imatani she is artist in residence at the City of Portland Archives and Records Center, commissioned by the Regional Arts and Culture Council, and they have collaborated on several installations, including at the Blaffer Art Museum in Houston as part of Antena Exhibition, the Killingsworth Branch of Multnomah Public Library, and in the Portland State University Recreation Building. Sand lives in Portland, Oregon, with Jules Boykoff and their daughter, Jessi Wahnetah, and she is currently working on a book on oil trains in the Pacific Northwest.

Leonard Schwartz is the author most recently of *IF* and *At Element*, both from Talisman House. Other books include *The Library of Seven Readings* (Ugly Duckling Presse) and *A Message Back and other Furors* (Chax). He teaches poetics at The Evergreen State College in Olympia, Washington.

Prageeta Sharma is a professor in the MFA program at the University of Montana in Missoula, where she has lived for the last seven years, and author of four poetry collections: *Bliss to Fill; The Opening Question; Infamous Landscapes* and *Undergloom*. In 2010 she received a Howard Foundation Grant. She is the founder and co-director (with poet Joanna Klink) of *Thinking Its Presence: Race, Creative Writing, and Literary Study*.

Jeremy Springsteed is a poet, painter, percussionist and barista living in Seattle, where he co-founded the Breadline performance series with Alex O. Bleecker and Greg Bem.

Marilyn Stablein, poet, essayist, collagist and book artist, is the author of twelve books. Her collection *Splitting Hard Ground* won the New Mexico Book Award and the National Federation of Press Women Book Award. Other books include *Sleeping in Caves: A Sixties Himalayan Memoir* and a collection of eco-essays, *Climate of Extremes: Landscape and Imagination*. Fiction collections include *Vermin: A Bestiary* and *The Census Taker: Tales of a Traveler in India and Nepal*. She and her husband own Anthology Booksellers, an independent used and out-of-print bookstore in Portland, Oregon, and online. Visit marilynstablein.com.

Sharon Thesen grew up in small towns across Western Canada, and for many years she taught English and Creative Writing at Capilano College in North Vancouver. Since 2005 she has taught in the Department of Creative Studies at UBC's Okanagan Campus and is now Professor Emeritus of Creative Writing. She is the editor of *The New Long Poem Anthology*, and was an editor of *The Capilano Review* and co-editor of *Lake: A Journal of Arts and Environment*. Her recent poetry books include *A Pair of Scissors, The Good Bacteria* and *Oyama Pink Shale*.

Lary Timewell is a North Vancouver poet who has returned from twenty years in Fukushima, Japan. Some of his most recent work has appeared in *The Capilano Review* and as the chapbook *tones employed as loss* from above/ground press.

Anastacia Tolbert's work is a syrupy rune—wings, words & why not. She is a Cave Canem Fellow, Hedgebrook Alumna, Jack Straw Writer, EDGE Professional Writer, VONA alum, creative writing workshop facilitator, documentarian and playwright. She is writer, co-director and co-producer of *Gotbreast?* (2007): a documentary about the views of women regarding breast and body image. Lately she's been obsessed with the body and the stories it holds. Her poetry, fiction and nonfiction have been published widely. http://www.anastaciatolbert.com/

Fred Wah, OC, was born in Swift Current, Saskatchewan, but grew up in the Kootenays in southeast British Columbia. He has published since the early 1960s and frequently presents internationally on Canadian poetry and poetics. Recent books are *Diamond Grill, a biofiction* (1996), *Faking It: Poetics and Hybridity,* a collection of essays (2000) and two collections of poetry, *Sentenced to Light* (Talonbooks, 2008) and *is a door* (Talonbooks, 2009). He is a former Parliamentary Poet Laureate.

Thomas Walton's work has appeared/will appear in *Bombay Gin, ZYZZYVA, Delmar, Cirque, Gambling the Aisle* and other journals. He's currently the editor of *PageBoy Magazine:* http://pageboymagazine.blogspot.com out of Seattle, WA.

Gillian Wigmore is the author of three books of poems: *soft geography* (Caitlin Press, 2007), winner of the 2008 ReLit Award, *Dirt of Ages* (Nightwood, 2012) and *Orient* (Brick Books, 2014), as well as a novella, *Grayling* (Mother Tongue Publishing, 2014). Her work has been published in magazines, shortlisted for prizes and anthologized. She lives in Prince George, BC.

Carletta Carrington Wilson is a visual and literary artist; her poems have appeared in *Pilgrimage; Cimarron Review; Obsidian III; Seattle Review; Raven Chronicles; The Journal: Book Club of Washington; Beyond the Frontier: African American Poetry for the 21st Century; Uncommon Waters: Women Write about Fishing* and *Seattle Poets and Photographers: A Millennium Reflection.* Her work has appeared online in *Torch* and *Rattapallax: Innovative Northwest Poets.*

Lissa Wolsak works at A United Lark ~ Energy Psychology in Vancouver, BC. She is a poet/essayist and author of *The Garcia Family Co-Mercy; Pen Chants, or nth or 12 Spirit-like Impermanences; A Defence of Being; An Heuristic Prolusion; Squeezed Light: Collected Works 1995–2004* from Station Hill of Barrytown, and forthcoming long poems *Thrall; Of Beings Alone ~ The Eigenface; P)light;* and *LIGHTSAIL.*

Rita Wong lives on the unceded Coast Salish territories of the Musqueam, Squamish and Tsleil-Waututh First Nations. Her newest book of poems, *undercurrent,* is being published by Nightwood Editions in 2015.

Maged Zaher was born and raised in Cairo, and currently lives in Seattle. He is the author of *If Reality Doesn't Work Out* (SplitLevel Text Press, 2014), *Thank You for the Window Office* (Ugly Duckling Presse, 2012), *The Revolution Happened and You Didn't Call Me* (Tinfish Press, 2012) and *Portrait of the Poet as an Engineer* (Pressed Wafer, 2009). His collaborative work with the Australian poet Pam Brown, *farout_library_ software,* was published by Tinfish Press in 2007. His translations of contemporary Egyptian poetry have appeared in *Jacket Magazine, Banipal* and *Denver Quarterly,* and are forthcoming as a book: *The Tahrir of Poems,* from Alice Blue Review. He performed his work at Subtext, Bumbershoot, the Kootenay School of Writing, St. Marks Project, Evergreen State College and The American University in Cairo. Maged is the recipient of the 2013 Genius Award in Literature from the Seattle weekly *The Stranger.*